T H O R E A U

THE QUEST AND THE CLASSICS

BY ETHEL SEYBOLD

ARCHON BOOKS
1969

Copyright, 1951, by Yale University Press
Reprinted 1969 with permission of Yale University Press
in an unaltered and unabridged edition

{*Yale Studies in English, Vol. 116*}

SBN: 208 00774 1
Library of Congress Catalog Card Number: 69-15691
Printed in the United States of America

To

MARY ANICE SEYBOLD

PREFACE

THIS study has gone through several stages in the process of becoming a book. It began as an investigation of the facts of Thoreau's classicism. But when it was possible to say exactly what kind of classicist Thoreau was, there arose a second question: why was he a classicist at all? Here was a man who disliked nonessentials. He had no use for personal property, for conventional society, or for idle learning; yet he took the *Iliad* with him to Walden. When a man who defined the cost of a thing as the amount of life one had to give in exchange for it was willing to spend "youthful days and costly hours" in classical study, it may be assumed that for some reason he found the classics indispensable. The investigation became then an attempt to find that reason by locating in his classical reading the specific foci of his interest and establishing their relationship to the experiences of his life and thought. With the answer to this problem came the solution to many other perplexing problems concerning Thoreau. Thoreau the classicist had been all the while Thoreau the man, exercising one of his partial functions; through the analysis of the partial function Thoreau the man was revealed: whole, consistent, and explicable in all his functions. For the reason for which Thoreau read the classics was also the reason which underlay all his activities, the quest to which he devoted his life. The quest took at last its proper place as the central theme of the book; Thoreau's classicism became important to the investigator in the same way in which it was important to Thoreau, as a tool in a greater investigation.

The book in its original form was presented to the faculty of the Graduate School of Yale University in candidacy for the degree of doctor of philosophy. My pleasure in writing it was increased by the generous assistance I received from many sources. I have acknowledged my debts in the proper places in the footnotes; I wish, however, to make certain acknowledgments here. I owe special gratitude to Houghton Mifflin, authorized publishers of Thoreau's works and publishers also of many books on Thoreau, for their permission to quote liberally from their publications. I am grateful for the use of collections of Thoreau manuscript: the Henry W. and Albert A. Berg Collection of the New York Public Library, and the collections in the Henry E. Huntington Library, the Pierpont Morgan Library, the Widener Memorial Library at Harvard University, and the Library of Congress. Kenneth Cameron's permission to use his identifications of the books which Thoreau borrowed from the Harvard Library saved me many hours of work. I owe much to Professor Stanley T. Williams, under whose direction the dissertation was written, for his steady help and encouragement through all the stages of the work and to Professor Benjamin C. Nangle for his valuable advice and suggestions in the final preparation of the manuscript.

E. S.

Illinois College
September 10, 1950

NOTES ON SOURCES

THE fundamental source of this book has been Thoreau's own writing, published and unpublished. For the bulk of the published writing I have used the twenty volumes of the Walden edition of Thoreau's works: Henry David Thoreau, *The Writings of Henry David Thoreau* (Walden edition, Boston, Houghton Mifflin, 1905). Of the single items which have been published since this edition, I have considered only fresh material, ignoring new combinations of what has already been published.

For the Walden edition I have adopted the short title *Writings,* followed by the volume number. When it has seemed pertinent and not unduly cumbersome I have added the name of the article or book or the date of the journal entry from which the reference came. I have used complete titles for articles or books except for Volume 1, *A Week on the Concord and Merrimack Rivers,* which I have called *The Week.* In the case of the journal entries Thoreau's varied systems of dating are responsible for variations in date form. He has dated some entries by year, month, and day; others less definitely.

There is Thoreau manuscript in the New York Public, the Morgan, the Harvard (both Houghton and Widener), the Abernethy (Middlebury College), the Henry E. Huntington, the Concord Free Public libraries, and in the Library of Congress. From these collections there are certain items which I have used repeatedly. I list them here with their location, a brief description of content, and the designations, either titles or manuscript numbers or both, by which they are known. In referring to manuscript in the text, I have preferred to use titles when they are familiar or descriptive ones; in the documentation I have used manuscript numbers when they were available.

Index Rerum
(*HM945*)

A large commonplace book in the Henry E. Huntington Library, San Marino, California. It contains material from 1836 to 1860 including among other things fragmentary indices to the journals, lists of subjects for composition, book reviews, material on Scott, quotations from Milton, and, of greatest interest to this study, Thoreau's own library list.

College Note-Book
(*MA. 594*)

A commonplace book in the Pierpont Morgan Library labeled by Thoreau "Miscellaneous Extracts, Cambridge, Mass, Nov. 1836." It contains sections on word derivation and language structure; much English poetry; a hodgepodge of philosophical reading in Cudworth, Zoroaster, the *Laws of Menu,* and the *Sayings of Mahomet;* and in the classics selections from Horace, Persius, and Plutarch.

HM13201

A forty-page commonplace book in the Huntington Library containing material from 1836 to 1841. Among early poems, journal indices, and opinions on education, there is a March, 1841, reading list.

Literary Note-Book

A large notebook in the Library of Congress. It can be dated approximately 1840–43. It contains 361 pages of varied material including selections from Chaucer and from the cavalier and metaphysical poets. The major classical quotation comes from Jamblichus' *Life of Pythagoras* and from the *Orphica.*

Harvard Fact-Book

A commonplace book of the 1850's in the Harry Elkins Widener Memorial Library at Harvard. This contains much nonclassical material on natural history and a brief selection from Lemprière's *Classical Dictionary.*

A Book of Extracts

A commonplace book of the last years of Thoreau's life, now in the Henry W. and Albert A. Berg Collection of the New York Public Library. It contains selections from Aristotle, Pliny, Theophrastus, Aelian, and Herodotus.

HM934

A manuscript in the Huntington Library containing seven of Thoreau's essays.

Manuscript Journals (MA. 1302)

These are in the Morgan Library. Certain parts have been omitted in the published version. The classical omissions are from the husbandry writers and from Strabo.

Huntington Journal Fragments (HM13182)

Journal fragments of the 1840's, supposedly held out by Sophia from the other journals and left with relatives. They are now in the Huntington Library. They contain rather personal comments on love and friendship. Among the fragments is a fifty-page journal of the Staten Island episode.

CONTENTS

THOREAU:

THE QUEST AND THE CLASSICS

I

Proteus

"The fact is I am a mystic, a transcendentalist, and a natural philosopher to boot."

CRITICISM has given us no integrated interpretation of Thoreau. Certain of his friends and early biographers came close to recognizing him for what he was but they made no statements precise and convincing enough to transmit their information. Nor have other critics been more successful. Too many have been willing to believe that "the whole of Thoreau, the objective and subjective man—is to be found in the two books he saw through the press."[1] Others have read the journals, but usually to "cull out the significant things here and there"[2] to prove their own special theses. And so we have Thoreau in one after another Protean disguise: Thoreau the hermit; Thoreau the naturalist; Thoreau the scholar, student of the classics, of oriental lore, of New England legend and history, of the life of the North American Indian; Thoreau the primitivist, the "apostle of the wild"; Thoreau the man of letters, writer of perfect prose; even Thoreau the walker.

Certainly Thoreau appeared in each of these roles, but his life is not explained by any one of them. And when we examine him closely in any one role we find always that he did not quite fit the part, that he exhibited certain peculiar aberrations and deficiencies: a partial, intermittent, temporary hermit, who spent a good part of two years in semiseclusion, who rather liked to eat out, who said of himself even, "I am naturally no hermit";[3] a naturalist whose ornithology was never quite trustworthy and who contributed no new fact of importance to natural history; a scholar who believed that men had a respect for scholarship much greater than its use and spoke of the great reproach of idle learning; a classicist who preferred the agricultural writers to the literary authors; a reader of oriental philosophy who genuinely disapproved of any system of

1. William Lyon Phelps, *Howells, James, Bryant, and Other Essays* (New York, Macmillan, 1924), p. 79.

2. John Burroughs, "Another Word on Thoreau," *The Last Harvest* (Boston and New York, Houghton Mifflin, 1922), p. 148.

3. *Writings*, II, 155.

philosophy; a student of New England history who found genealogy ridiculous and the facts of history unimportant; an expert on the North American Indian whose experience came largely from books, from Joe Polis, and from gathering arrowheads while the red man still roamed the West; a primitivist who might talk of devouring a raw woodchuck but who also talked of abstaining from animal food; a man of letters who published little and was relieved when it did not sell; a writer who believed that a man's life was the perfect communication; a walker of whom Emerson said that if he did not walk he could not write but who spent his last months in composition and never even referred to his former outdoor life.

Certainly Thoreau was not basically or primarily any one of these. Was he then simply a Jack-of-all-trades, interested superficially or whimsically in a wide variety of things—or, in more complimentary terms, a man of extreme versatility? For there does not seem at first sight any way to reconcile such apparently divergent interests as his. John King, the classicist, was surprised that a man could love both Homer and nature, and although we may group together the hermit, the primitive, and the Indian lover, what common denominator can we find, say, for the classics and the North American Indian? In the face of such difficulties it has become a habit for scholars to conclude that Thoreau is an enigma and his life full of paradoxes. Yet judgment revolts against that conclusion. If we know Henry Thoreau at all, we are convinced that there was no contradiction within the man himself and that he lived no aimless life of shifting interest and activity, but that here was a man with a purpose in his life, one who knew what he was about and who went steadily and persistently about it.

He spoke often of the value and necessity of a serious occupation. He knew himself seriously occupied and was annoyed that others did not seem to realize it. His working hours were inviolable. Why should a huckleberry party feel that he had leisure to join the excursion simply because he was not shut up in a school room?[4] Could not his friends understand the impossibility of interrupting his work in order to visit them? "Not that I could not enjoy such visits, if I were not otherwise occupied. I have enjoyed very much my visits to you . . . and am sorry that I cannot enjoy such things oftener; but life is short, and there are other things also to be done."[5] Especially as he grew older did he feel the shortness of life and the pressure of work. "I have many affairs to attend to, and feel hurried these days."[6]

These affairs were part of a single, lifelong enterprise. In "Life without Principle," completed in the last year of Thoreau's life, he gave

4. *Ibid.*, XVIII, 333; journal of September 16, 1859.
5. *Ibid.*, VI, 353; letter to Daniel Ricketson, November 4, 1860.
6. *Ibid.*, XVIII, 344; journal of September 24, 1859.

testimony to the fact that he had known what he would do with his life even before he was of proper age to carry out his project. Marveling again that men could often have supposed him idle and unoccupied, available for their trivial undertakings, he corrected the error: "No, no! I am not without employment at this stage of the voyage. To tell the truth, I saw an advertisement for able-bodied seamen, when I was a boy, sauntering in my native port, and as soon as I came of age I embarked."[7]

But for what port, or by what route, is not so clearly stated. Thoreau referred obliquely and mysteriously to the nature of his enterprise in such public announcements as *The Week* and *Walden:* "I cut another furrow than you see,"[8] and "If I should attempt to tell how I have desired to spend my life in years past, it would probably surprise those of my readers who are somewhat acquainted with its actual history; it would certainly astonish those who know nothing about it. I will only hint at some of the enterprises which I have cherished."[9]

He would have liked to tell the world what he was doing, had it been possible: ". . . there are more secrets in my trade than in most men's, and yet not voluntarily kept, but inseparable from its very nature. I would gladly tell all that I know about it, and never paint 'No Admittance' on my gate."[1] Certainly he tried hard enough to communicate with his friends. He was even willing, he said, "to pass for a fool" in his "desperate, perhaps foolish, efforts to persuade them to lift the veil from off the possible and future, which they hold down with both their hands, before their eyes."[2] Communication involves comprehension as well as expression.

It was, as we should expect, only in the private record of the journal that Thoreau made a plain statement of his business in life. He had been asked by the Association for the Advancement of Science to state that branch of science in which he was particularly interested. He complained that he would not be taken seriously were he to make a public confession.

. . . I felt that it would be to make myself the laughing-stock of the scientific community to describe . . . that branch of science . . . inasmuch as they do not believe in a science which deals with the higher law. So I was obliged to speak to their condition and describe to them that poor part of me which alone they can understand. The fact is I am a mystic, a transcendentalist, and a natural philosopher to boot. Now that I think of it, I should have told them at once that I was a transcendentalist. That would have been the shortest way of telling them that they would not understand my explanations.[3]

He was right in saying that the scientists would not understand him if he called himself a mystic, a transcendentalist, and a natural philosopher. Burroughs even misunderstood the last term, assuming that

7. *Ibid.,* iv, 460. 8. *Ibid.,* i, 54. 9. *Ibid.,* ii, 18. i. *Ibid.*
2. *Ibid.,* xv, 495; journal of July 29, 1857.
3. *Ibid.,* xi, 4; journal of March 5, 1853.

Thoreau meant naturalist or natural historian, which was certainly not his thought, as anyone who has read the endless distinctions between poet and scientist in the journals of the 1850's should know. But Thoreau might well have widened the class of scientists, for often as these words have been quoted, many earnest students of Thoreau are still refusing to take them earnestly. We regard them as an instance of Thoreau's perversity and exaggeration, qualities always to be dealt with in trying to find Thoreau. Or, identifying transcendentalism with Hawthorne's mist, moonshine, and raw potatoes, we simply refuse to believe that anyone who seems as practical and down to earth as Thoreau could be in any real sense transcendental. But Thoreau was not afraid to wear the label or to defend the faith, even to defend its practicality. He talks about lecturing on the subject of reality "rather transcendentally treated."[4] He understands that people complain that his lectures are transcendental, but he comments caustically that if you call a lecture "Education" the audience will pronounce it good, while if you call it "Transcendentalism" the same audience will find it moonshine.[5] As for his outward appearance of practicality, he warns that it cannot be trusted; pushed too far, "I begin to be transcendental and show where my heart is."[6] And in more serious vein he asserts repeatedly that the practicality of the world is delusion and the so-called impracticality of the poet, the philosopher, the transcendentalist is the only true practicality. The values of the banker are subject to fluctuation; the poet's values are permanent. Who would be willing to "exchange an absolute and infinite value for a relative and finite one,—to gain the whole world and lose his own soul!"[7]

It is worth noting that Thoreau calls John Brown a practical man and a transcendentalist: "A man of rare common sense and directness of speech, as of action; a transcendentalist above all, a man of ideas and principles,—that was what distinguished him. Not yielding to whim or transient impulse, but carrying out the purpose of a life."[8]

But probably the major obstacle in the way of our accepting Thoreau's own definitive statement of himself is that the word "transcendentalist" does not constitute for us a definition. It says either too little or too much. There were, of course, all degrees and grades of transcendentalists just as there are all varieties of Christians. We classify as Christians all those who profess a Protestant or Catholic faith; we apply the term to good men, churchgoers, those who abstain from the major vices. So do we classify as transcendentalists all to whom transcendentalism meant nothing more than a new and hopeful view of life, permitting them to substitute a god of love for a god of wrath, the dignity of the soul for natural

4. *Ibid.,* VI, 189; letter to T. W. Higginson, April 2–3, 1852.
5. *Ibid.,* XIX, 145; journal of February 13, 1860. See also *ibid.,* XIII, 197.
6. *Ibid.,* VIII, 228; journal of June 7, 1851. See also *ibid.,* VI, 32, 81.
7. *Ibid.,* VI, 216; letter to Harrison Blake, February 27, 1853. See also *ibid.,* XX, 283–4.
8. *Ibid.,* IV, 413; "A Plea for Captain John Brown."

depravity, conscience for law, and the warm sense of personal conviction for the emptiness of the unknown and unknowable. We think of "Christian" specifically in connection with the professionally religious: ministers, Sunday-school superintendents, missionaries. In the same way when we say "transcendental" we think at once of such leaders of the movement as Emerson and Alcott, preachers and missionaries of the faith, those who wrote the sermons and carried the gospel into the wilderness of the West. Used in such ways the terms must be rejected as definitive or identifying; they are only vaguely descriptive.

Both words have, however, real meanings, meanings which we almost never use because they seem to us impossibilities. Thoreau spoke of the wide gap between the accepted and the real meanings of the word "Christian" and of the difficulty of finding a real Christian. "It is not every man who can be a Christian," he said, "even in a very moderate sense . . ."[9] And speaking of the New Testament, the embodiment of Christian doctrine, he commented thus:

I know of no book that has so few readers. There is none so truly strange, and heretical, and unpopular. To Christians, no less than Greeks and Jews, it is foolishness and a stumbling block. There are, indeed, severe things in it which no man should read aloud more than once. "Seek first the kingdom of heaven." "Lay not up for yourselves treasures on earth." "If thou wilt be perfect, go and sell that thou hast, and give to the poor, and thou shalt have treasure in heaven." "For what is a man profited, if he shall gain the whole world, and lose his own soul? Or what shall a man give in exchange for his soul?" Think of this, Yankees! "Verily, I say unto you, if ye have faith as a grain of mustard seed, ye shall say unto this mountain, Remove hence to yonder place, and it shall remove; and nothing shall be impossible unto you." Think of repeating these things to a New England audience! . . . They never *were* read, they never *were* heard.[1]

Where is the Christian who does these things? Where is the man who believes enough to practice? Call a man a Christian in this sense, and no one will credit the statement.

So we have refused again and again to credit Thoreau's statement that he was a transcendentalist. In one sense it means nothing; in another it is incredible; we ignore it. We are no different in this respect from his friends, who consistently ignored and denied the significance of his life, insisting on seeing "parts, not wholes." Alcott said of him, "He is less thinker than observer; a naturalist in tendency but of a mystic habit, and a genius for detecting the essence in the form and giving forth the soul of things seen."[2] But the terms are in reverse order; Thoreau was a mystic first and a naturalist second.

9. *Ibid.*, IV, 445; "The Last Days of John Brown."
1. *Ibid.*, I, 73–4; *The Week*.
2. *The Journals of Bronson Alcott,* ed. Odell Shepard (Boston, Little, Brown, 1938), p. 318; journal of July 3, 1859.

Sanborn could see all the parts of Thoreau and refuse to state the whole: ". . . Thoreau, though a naturalist by habit, and a moralist by constitution, was inwardly a poet . . . His mind tended naturally to the ideal side."[3] "Thoreau's business in life was observation, thought, and writing, to which last, reading was essential."[4] Such statements are reminiscent of one of Thoreau's own: "Have not we our everlasting life to get? and is not that the only excuse at last for eating, drinking, sleeping, or even carrying an umbrella when it rains?"[5] His friends could see him eating, drinking, sleeping, even carrying the familiar umbrella through the woods, but they could not perceive that he was "getting his everlasting life." They could say that the business of his life was reading, observation, thought, and writing; they could recognize him as naturalist, poet, mystic; but they refused, even in that credulous and optimistic time, to add up the terms. They, like us, did not believe in real Christians or real transcendentalists.

But it was in the real meaning of the term that Thoreau called himself a transcendentalist. He said it as one might say, "I am a bricklayer." It was the occupation of his days and the pattern of his life. He was that rare phenomenon, a practitioner of his faith. *"Philosophia practica est eruditionis meta,"* he quoted, "Philosophy practiced is the goal of learning . . ."[6] And again, "We are shown fair scenes in order that we may be tempted to inhabit them, and not simply tell what we have seen."[7] Transcendental doctrine showed him fair scenes and he meant to dwell in them. He made in *Walden* a clear distinction between himself and his fellow transcendentalists in his distinction between philosophers and professors of philosophy.

There are nowadays professors of philosophy, but not philosophers. . . . To be a philosopher is not merely to have subtle thoughts, nor even to found a school, but so to love wisdom as to live . . . a life of simplicity, independence, magnanimity, and trust. It is to solve some of the problems of life, not only theoretically, but practically.[8]

Why should not a man's faith determine his work? Newspaper editors might think John Brown insane because he believed himself divinely appointed for his work, but

They talk as if it were impossible that a man could be "divinely appointed" in these days to do any work whatever; as if vows and religion were out of date as connected with any man's daily work . . .[9]

---

3. F. B. Sanborn, *Henry D. Thoreau,* ed. Charles Dudley Warner, "American Men of Letters Series" (Boston and New York, Houghton Mifflin, 1891), p. 284.

4. *Ibid.,* p. 300.

5. *Writings,* VI, 214; letter to Harrison Blake, February 27, 1853.

6. *Ibid.,* IV, 344; "Thomas Carlyle and his Works."

7. *Ibid.,* XVI, 202; journal of November 24, 1857.

8. *Ibid.,* II, 16.

9. *Ibid.,* IV, 436; "A Plea for Captain John Brown."

What is more urgent for any man than the attainment of the great and certain promises?

Yet the man who does not betake himself at once and desperately to sawing is called a loafer, though he may be knocking at the doors of heaven all the while, which shall surely be opened to him.[1]

Why should it be impossible for a man to *know?*

Surely, we are provided with senses as well fitted to penetrate the spaces of the real, the substantial, the eternal, as these outward are to penetrate the material universe.[2]

The truth, the quite incredible truth about Thoreau, the truth that we resist in spite of his own repeated witness, is that he spent a quarter of a century in a quest for transcendent reality, in an attempt to discover the secret of the universe. It is, after all, a matter only of belief. If one believed that the riddle could be solved, the mystery penetrated, the secret laid bare, who would choose to remain in ignorance? Thoreau believed; he accepted the conditions;[3] he claimed the promises. He had the map to the hidden treasure, and his whole life was spent in the search. Only when we see him and his life in this light do the pieces of the puzzle fall into place; his divergent interests are reconciled and all his paradoxes are resolved by the simple fact of his transcendentalism.

It is unnecessary to be scholarly or philosophical about transcendentalism. We are not concerned with its sources, system, and influences; only with its general pattern in New England in Thoreau's time. The best place to find what transcendentalism meant to its followers is the *Dial,*[4] the little family journal, the quarterly round robin which held them all together, which sounded the message of encouragement to the initiate and the advertisement of hope to the rest of the world. Thoreau expressed what the *Dial* meant to him in a letter to Emerson written from New York in 1843: "I hear the sober and the earnest, the sad and the cheery voices of my friends, and to me it is a long letter of encouragement and reproof; and no doubt so it is to many another in the land."[5]

The message it carried to its readers was simple, and simply and fervently, although somewhat repetitiously, stated. It proclaimed belief

---

1. *Ibid.,* x, 433; journal of December 28, 1852.
2. *Ibid.,* ii, 412; *The Week.*
3. The conditions were solitude, poverty, and the public opprobrium of failure and possibly of insanity. See *Writings,* viii, 11: "Referred to the world's standard, the hero, the discoverer, is insane, its greatest men are all insane." One of the reasons we have been slow to admit the truth about Thoreau is that it seems to us the equivalent of calling him "insane."
4. Read particularly "The Editors to the Reader," *Dial,* Vol. i, No. 1 (July, 1840); "Prophecy—Transcendentalism—Progress," *ibid.,* Vol. ii, No. 1 (July, 1841); and Emerson's "Lectures on the Times," *ibid.,* Vol. iii, Nos. 1-3 (July, October, 1842; January, 1843). The summary and all quoted phraseology come from these articles.
5. *Writings,* vi, 94; letter to Emerson, July 8, 1843.

in an all-good Creator who wished to be accessible to all his creatures, who made no special revelations to special groups, entrusting the truth to any exclusive religion or philosophy, but who kept the channel of communication open from himself to every soul. The soul was able of itself to recognize and communicate with the Spirit of which it was made, to perceive the infinite and absolute, to understand its own relation "to all being and all eternity." Since every soul must possess this power, it was not a matter of sense perception or of logic or intellect but a matter of intuition. Man had only to seek God in solitude, reverence, and faith in order to find him. Every man was potentially a mystic.

Within man himself, then, lay all the answers, but not in man alone. Man was only part of the creation, and the pattern and principles of the universe existed in every part, had so existed always and everywhere, in the commonest phenomenon of nature and the smallest unit of matter. Essentially nature never changed, and if man would know the secret of the universe he had only to observe her "visible aspects." Insight and sympathy would show him "the unseen in the visible, the ideal in the actual," the real and eternal creation behind the apparent and temporary. He who so observed and discovered might be called a natural philosopher. But whether through mysticism or through nature, when a man discerned "the open secret of the universe" he then became "a prophet, a seer of the future," and his utterance was inspired. The word "prophet" was synonymous with the word "poet." Poet or prophet possessed not only "the gift of insight" but "the faculty of communication, instruction, persuasion . . . a profound faith, and earnest eloquence . . ." Not only did the poet know, but it was his function to speak.

There have been such men in all ages, men who perceived truth and transmitted it. Moses was such a man to the Hebrews, and Orpheus and Homer to the Greeks and "through them to all modern civilization." The great books of all cultures contain the fragments and glimpses of truth revealed to their authors. Yet, however valuable these may be as guides, the final test of truth lies in the individual soul. Every man should be poet.

When we try the pattern to Thoreau, it fits.

A hermit? Not at all; but one who needed solitude, the solitude that was the primary requirement of the poet, the solitude essential for the mystic state in which revelation comes. This insistence upon solitude was so characteristic of youthful transcendentalists that Emerson expressed a mild regret that so many promising young people should feel the necessity of withdrawal and retreat.[6] It was so much a commonplace of the times that it made the plot of Ellery Channing's half-autobiographical narrative, *The Youth of the Poet and the Painter,* in which the hero, like his author, escapes from college and establishes himself

6. "The Transcendentalist," *Dial,* iii, No. 1, 303–4.

in a rural retreat, to the bewilderment of his devoted but conventional family and to his own great satisfaction.[7] This epistolary novel was published in the *Dial* during the year when Thoreau was doing much of the editing and may possibly have given energy to his already expressed desire to withdraw to Walden. Not a hermit, but a mystic.

Not a naturalist, but a natural philosopher. Thoreau was very jealous of the distinction and expressed it over a period of many years at great length and in a variety of ways. "Man cannot afford to be a naturalist," he announced flatly, "to look at Nature directly, but only with the side of his eye. He must look through and beyond her."[8] Emerson contributed much to Thoreau's reputation as a naturalist, but Emerson did not know very clearly what a naturalist was; and Burroughs, who did know, also knew that Thoreau was not one.

Emerson says Thoreau's determination on natural history was organic, but it was his determination on supernatural history that was organic. . . . Thoreau was not a born naturalist, but a born supernaturalist. . . . The natural history in his books is quite secondary. . . . He was more intent on the natural history of his own thought than on that of the bird. . . . he was looking too intently for a bird behind the bird—for a mythology to shine through his ornithology.[9]

Burroughs knew that Thoreau was looking for something, but being no more a natural philosopher than Emerson was a naturalist, he was never quite certain what it was: "He cross-questions the stumps and the trees as if searching for the clue to some important problem, but no such problem is disclosed. . . . In fact, his journal is largely the record of a search for something he never fully finds . . ."[1]

He was searching, of course, for that true and ideal world of which this is but the reflection, and Burroughs made a more accurate statement than he perhaps realized when he said, "Natural history was but one of the doors through which he sought to gain admittance to this inner and finer heaven of things."[2]

Scholarship was another door, for the utterances of other poets and prophets were the third avenue to truth. Histories, chronologies, traditions were all "written revelations."[3] Some poet might already have found, might at any time find, what he had missed.

The book exists for us, perchance, which will explain our miracles and reveal new ones. The at present unutterable things we may find somewhere uttered.

7. *Dial*, Vol. IV, Nos. 1–4 (July, 1843–April, 1844).
8. *Writings*, XI, 45; journal of March 23, 1853.
9. John Burroughs, "Henry D. Thoreau," *Indoor Studies* (Boston and New York, Houghton Mifflin, 1893), and "Another Word on Thoreau," *The Last Harvest, passim.*
1. *Ibid.*
2. Burroughs, "Henry D. Thoreau," *op. cit.*, p. 33. Burroughs' antecedent for "inner and finer heaven of things" is vague. It seems to be "supernatural history."
3. *Writings*, II, 342; *Walden*.

These same questions that disturb and puzzle and confound us have in their turn occurred to all the wise men; not one has been omitted; and each has answered them, according to his ability, by his words and his life.[4]

The last phrase is also significant. The lives of great men were as interesting to Thoreau as their books. He wished to know how they lived. In fact, he seemed often to investigate a man's life before he read his works; the commonplace books record biography before they record quotation.

But books were not only "the simplest and purest channel by which a revelation may be transmitted from age to age";[5] they served a second use, as a check on one's own experience. The poor hired man who had had "his second birth and peculiar religious experience" might know that Zoroaster, "thousands of years ago, travelled the same road and had the same experience," and might thus be assured of the authenticity and universality of his own.[6] Thoreau himself spoke of searching books for confirmation of the reality of his own experiences.[7]

Thoreau's reading, aside from that in natural history, falls into certain clearly marked categories: the Greek and Latin classics, the oriental scriptures, the English poets, New England history and legend, data on the North American Indian, and early accounts of travel, adventure, and exploration. It would be difficult to say in which field he read most or which he enjoyed most, but anyone who has read *Walden* will be aware that he valued the classics most. "For what are the classics but the noblest recorded thoughts of man? They are the only oracles which are not decayed, and there are such answers to the most modern inquiry in them as Delphi and Dodona never gave." [8]

The oriental scriptures also had a high place in his esteem. They, like the classics, were required reading for the transcendentalist, and one of Thoreau's chores for the *Dial* was the arrangement of collections of oriental quotations and sayings. Their elements of mysticism and contemplation naturally appealed to him; but probably the source of their greatest interest for him was the same as it was in the case of Orpheus and Homer—their antiquity. "They seem to have been uttered," he said, "with a sober morning prescience, in the dawn of time."[9]

All antiquities had a great attraction for Thoreau. They seemed to him not so much old as early, not so far removed from the present as near to the beginning. There is, to be sure, a slight inconsistency between the belief that all things are everywhere and always the same and the suspicion that the further back you are in time, the closer you are to

4. *Ibid.*, II, 120; *Walden.*   5. *Ibid.*, VII, 370; journal of 1845.
6. *Ibid.*, II, 120; *Walden.*
7. *Ibid.*, VIII, 307; journal of July 16, 1851.
8. *Ibid.*, II, 112; *Walden.*
9. *Ibid.*, VII, 277; journal of August 30, 1841. For slight variant of this statement see *ibid.*, I, 155; *The Week.*

reality. But that suspicion was always with Thoreau. He fancied that the message shone a little clearer in the beginning.

English poetry he found derivative, imitative, and tame, lacking "the rudeness and vigor of youth." It was characteristic that he should approve Chaucer most, since he might be regarded as "the Homer of the English poets" and "the youthfullest of them all."[1] But despite his extensive reading in the field and his frequent quotation, he was more inclined to be critical than admiring, going so far even as to wonder whether he might not have contracted a lethargy from his attempt to read straight through Chalmers' *English Poets!*[2]

Thoreau's concern with the primitive was only another manifestation of his interest in antiquities. Primitive man is not necessarily old in time, but he is young in nature, which amounted to the same thing for Thoreau. He was delighted to find in Maine a man living "in the primitive age of the world, a primitive man. . . . He lives three thousand years deep into time, an age not yet described by poets. Can you well go further back in history than this?" he asks.[3] Therien, the woodchopper, fascinated him, as did Rice, the mountaineer, and Joe Polis, the Indian guide, descendant of still more primitive man. As the early man must have been closer to his Creator and to direct revelation, so the primitive or natural man must be closer to nature and to natural insight. Thoreau said of the Indian, "By the wary independence and aloofness of his dim forest life he preserves his intercourse with his native gods, and is admitted from time to time to a rare and peculiar society with Nature. He has glances of starry recognition to which our saloons are strangers."[4]

Thoreau found the same satisfaction in the study of the early history of the American colonies. When he read such books as John Smith's *General Historie of Virginia* he thought himself "in a wilder country, and a little nearer to primitive times."[5] Reading Wood's *New England's Prospect,* he remarked, "Certainly that generation stood nearer to nature, nearer to the facts, than this, and hence their books have more life in them."[6]

He believed that the truest accounts of things were given by those who saw them first,[7] and for that reason he enjoyed the early naturalists, explorers, and travelers. Within himself he tried to feel the sensations of earlier man and earlier times. He cultivated his own wildness. The scent of the Dicksonia fern translated him to the Silurian Period.[8] The sight of a toadstool carried him "back to the era of the formation of the

1. *Ibid.,* I, 395, 393; *The Week.*   2. *Ibid.,* II, 285; *Walden.*
3. *Ibid.,* III, 87; "Ktaadn."   4. *Ibid.,* I, 55; *The Week.*
5. *Ibid.,* X, 494; journal of February 23, 1853.
6. *Ibid.,* XIII, 109; journal of January 9, 1855.
7. *Ibid.,* XV, 232; journal of January 27, 1857.
8. *Ibid.,* XVIII, 346–7; journal of September 24, 1859.

coal-measures—the age of the saurus and pleiosaurus and when bull-frogs were as big as bulls."[9] He might become one with God through the mystic trance; he might become one with nature by surrendering himself completely to natural influences, by becoming himself a primitive man.

He was trying always to get back to the beginning of things, to "anticipate, not the sunrise and the dawn merely, but, if possible, Nature herself!"[1] There surely he would find the answer. The last years of his life found him reading Herodotus and Strabo, the one commonly classified as a historian, the other as a geographer, but he did not read them for the history of nations or the geography of countries; he read them for the history of the human race and the geography of the globe. That was as far back as he could go.

Thoreau's philological interests should be classified as scholarly. He made charts of the language families; he collected dictionaries of foreign languages, even Rasle's dictionary of the Abenaki tongue; he spoke often of the value of language training; his writing is full of speculation about word derivation and meaning, classical, Anglo-Saxon, French, Indian. But he was very skeptical about the learning of languages per se; his interest in words and languages was transcendental, semantic rather than etymological:

Talk about learning our *letters* and being literate! Why, the roots of *letters* are *things*. Natural objects and phenomena are the original symbols or types which express our thoughts and feelings . . .[2]

As in the expression of moral truths we admire any closeness to the physical fact which in all languages is the symbol of the spiritual, so, finally, when natural objects are described, it is an advantage if words derived originally from nature, it is true, but which have been turned (*tropes*) from their primary signification to a moral sense, are used . . .[3]

With Emerson's little diagram in his head and a dictionary—more often Latin than any other language—in his hand, he went looking for spiritual facts.

Not a writer merely—but a poet, he who receives and communicates the truth. The paradox of a man of letters who published so little is solved. If all that a man writes must be truth, his production will be limited. In his youth Thoreau felt very strongly the poet's obligation to make his report: "An honest book's the noblest work of man. It will do the world no good, hereafter, if you merely exist, and pass life smoothly or roughly; but to have thoughts, and write them down, that helps greatly."[4]

9. *Ibid.*, xi, 271; journal of June 18, 1853.   1. *Ibid.*, ii, 19; *Walden.*
2. *Ibid.*, xviii, 389; journal of October 16, 1859.
3. *Ibid.*, xix, 145; journal of February 15, 1860.
4. *Ibid.*, vi, 31; letter to his sister Helen, January 23, 1840.

Thoreau's endless revision served two purposes: to clarify his thoughts and experiences in his own mind, reducing them to their essence, and to eliminate rather than to achieve style. This also was transcendental conviction: ". . . the matter is all in all, and the manner nothing at all."[5] So strenuously did he try to reduce the communication to essentials that he could finally say, "the theme is nothing, the life is everything."[6] This idea that the life, the force, the vitality which the communication carried was all important is very close to Thoreau's speculation whether truth was not simply sincere being and living its only perfect communication.

A walker? Yes, but not so much a walker in Walden Woods as a saunterer to the Holy Land. In "Walking" it was not the physical act which was his subject. "We would fain take that walk, never yet taken by us through this actual world, which is perfectly symbolical of the path which we love to travel in the interior and ideal world . . ."[7] His walking was the material manifestation of his journey through life, his quest for "the other world" which was, as he said, "all my art."[8]

And so at last we see him whole: Thoreau, practicing transcendentalist. His solitude, his natural history, his scholarship, his writing, his walking were not ends but instruments. He forged them well and kept them sharp, but he frequently laid down one to pick up another, and he used them practically and efficiently toward one end only and without concern for other uses which they might serve.

If we cannot believe either Thoreau's repeated statements or the evidence of our own logical demonstration, we have another and better proof, that which Thoreau considered the perfect communication: the life of the man himself. "Some men's lives are but an aspiration, a yearning toward a higher state, and they are wholly misapprehended until they are referred to, or traced through all their metamorphoses."[9] There is only one way to trace Thoreau's life and that is through the journals. If we have misapprehended the life it is quite possibly because we have misapprehended the journals. They are not notebooks from which the best has been extracted. They are not, as Burroughs would have them, "merely negative," without human interest, a mass of irrelevant details. They are not, intrinsically, *Early Spring in Massachusetts*. They are a man's spiritual autobiography, a "record of experiences and growth,"[1] addressed to himself and to the gods.[2] "Is not the poet bound

5. *Ibid.*, IX, 86; journal of November 1, 1851.

6. *Ibid.*, XV, 121; journal of October 18, 1856.

7. *Ibid.*, V, 216–17.

8. *Ibid.*, I, xxiii; Emerson in his biographical sketch of Thoreau quotes him as saying in his youth, "The other world is all my art: my pencils will draw no other; my jackknife will cut nothing else . . ."

9. *Ibid.*, IX, 71; journal of October 14, 1851.

1. *Ibid.*, XIV, 134; journal of January 24, 1856.

2. *Ibid.*, XVII, 120; journal of August 23, 1858; IX, 107; VII, 206–7.

to write his own biography?" he asks, "Is there any other work for
him but a good journal?"[3]

It is not a "circumstantial" journal, one that deals with fact and
deed, with the trivia of everyday life, but a "substantial" one of truth
and thought; yet not the truth and thought of the public documents,
modified, simplified, and presented as conclusions, but truth and thought
in the process of evolution. In the journal we can follow Thoreau on
every step of his expedition, through one experiment after another, accumulating evidence, testing theories, building hypotheses. We can see
him hopeful, disappointed, successful, desperate, acquiescent.

We can follow him better if we adopt for our use one of the instruments by which he implemented his investigation. It would be difficult
to say which of these was his favorite, which he used most, or which
he found most efficient. Probably he would have considered the mystic
state the truest means of discovering reality, and quite likely he would
have placed the study of nature second. But mysticism belonged largely
to the period of his youth, and his recorded observation of nature especially to the decade after Walden. If we choose one of these we cannot
use it to full advantage throughout his life. There was a tool, however,
a phase of his scholarship, which he used in youth and in age and to the
value of which he gave frequent enthusiastic testimony, both public and
private; this was his classicism. There were intervals in his life, it is
true, when he did not read in the classics, but these were intervals
when he was not actively engaged in the quest, when it seemed to him
either that he might have reached his goal or that he had lost his way.
The classics seem never to have been absent from his thought.

Thoreau's classicism recommends itself for our use not only for these
reasons but also because it has not been so thoroughly analyzed as have
most of Thoreau's other channels of investigation. It has, indeed, usually been either exaggerated or ignored. Thoreau's contemporaries, out
of their admiration for him and their ignorance of the classics, and possibly because of their failure to recognize his real distinction and their
eagerness to create a distinction for him, made for him impossible claims,
crediting him with reading the works of authors whose works exist only
in scattered fragments in secondary sources and assuming that he read
and admired every work which he even mentioned. Later critics, no
doubt bewildered by a man who considered flour, sugar, and lard lux-
uries but regarded the *Iliad* as a necessity, have been content to leave the
subject alone and to generalize vaguely from the statements of their
predecessors.[4] It will be instructive, therefore, to make some preliminary

3. *Ibid.*, XVI, 115; journal of October 21, 1857.
4. Clarence Gohdes, "Henry Thoreau, Bachelor of Arts," *Classical Journal*, XXIII
(February, 1928), 323 ff., and Norman Foerster, "The Intellectual Heritage of Thoreau,"
Texas Review, II (April, 1917), 192 ff., have made commendably factual, although brief
and general, statements on Thoreau's classicism.

examination of the nature, scope, and quality of Thoreau's classicism.

We have already said the fundamental thing about the purpose of Thoreau's classical reading: that the classics were to him the most pertinent and valuable source of past revelation. It is possible to identify most of the classical works which Thoreau either owned or read not only by author and title but even by exact edition;[5] and it is possible through a study of his classical quotation, reference, and comment to discover what authors and subjects he found of special interest, what ideas and concepts appealed to him, and what influence the classics left upon his writing.[6] In brief summary we can say here that his postcollege reading fell generally into three periods. The first was a literary period; he began by rereading authors which he had read in college and by making little explorations into fields suggested by that reading. Among the Greeks he read Homer[7] and Orpheus;[8] the Greek lyrists, especially Anacreon and Pindar; in drama, Aeschylus' *Prometheus Bound* and *Seven against Thebes*. He investigated also Plutarch's *Lives* and *Morals,* Jamblichus' *Life of Pythagoras,* and Porphyry's *On Abstinence from Animal Food.* Among the Latin authors he read Vergil, Horace, Persius, and Ovid. In the second period, after *Walden,* in the

5. Appendix A of this work contains bibliographical identification of the classical books which it is known that Thoreau either owned or read. Identification of each book is accompanied by a description of content and by any information available on the disposition of the book after Thoreau's death or on its present location. Books are arranged chronologically in the order of Thoreau's acquisition or use, which is also the general order of their discussion in the text. The reader is urged to consult Appendix A for specific information on any classical book mentioned in the text as used or owned by Thoreau.

6. Appendix B of this work lists and identifies quotation in the published works of the major classical authors which Thoreau read. It includes quotation from Thoreau manuscript when such quotation adds anything to the knowledge of Thoreau's classicism. Authors are arranged alphabetically, and the quotations are arranged chronologically by date of use. The reader is urged to refer to this appendix for more specific and complete information than is admissible to text discussion.

Appendix C is a classical index to the published works of Thoreau. The reader can, by using this index, locate all classical translation, quotation, or reference made by Thoreau in the twenty volumes of his *Writings.*

7. How much reading Thoreau did in the *Odyssey* is debatable. It was the *Iliad* which he studied at Harvard, and it is the *Iliad* from which nearly all his references and quotations come. While in college he withdrew from the library an English translation of both the *Iliad* and the *Odyssey* (see App. A, No. 24); but his only quotation from the *Odyssey* (see App. B, "Homer") occurs in "Wild Apples" and is almost certainly taken from a secondary source; his references (see App. C) would not necessarily involve reading. The current popularity of the *Odyssey* as a source of literary themes did not prevail in Thoreau's time.

8. Orpheus was regarded by the Greeks as one of the inventors of music and poetry. He was mentioned as early as the sixth century B.C. as a historical rather than a mythological figure. A number of poems were attributed to him and collected by later writers. These, dating at least as far back as the fifth century, were collected along with a far greater number of Alexandrine forgeries under Orpheus' name and were until recently accepted as the genuine productions of one man. It was this collection of largely spurious items, now known as the pseudo-Orpheus, which Thoreau read.

early 1850's, he made the acquaintance of the agricultural writers, Cato, Varro, Columella, and Palladius, and confined himself to them with two exceptions, Sophocles' *Antigone* and a brief excursion into Lucretius. He did no new reading in Greek during this period.[9] In the late 1850's he discovered the early naturalists: the Roman Pliny and among the Greeks, Aristotle, Theophrastus, and Aelian. His last reading was in Herodotus and Strabo.[1]

Such reading is not standard classical fare; it is a personal selection directed toward Thoreau's special purpose. The basis of selection is not so obvious in the first period as in the later ones, but the young investigator had to begin where he was with what he knew. He was misled also by general literary ambition during the *Dial* days, but he quickly eliminated certain authors who did not fulfill his requirements. Persius he found lacking in the true poetical qualities, and he referred to his reading of Persius as "almost the last regular service which I performed in the cause of literature."[2] He wished that Pindar were "better worth translating."[3] Homer and Orpheus had for him the common attraction of their antiquity, Orpheus of an immeasurable antiquity. Each had besides his special attraction: Orpheus, mysticism; Homer, myth and nature. The Greek lyrics appealed to him simply as music, fine, remote, delicate, the true accompaniment of true poetry, the music of the spheres, the singing of the blood, the ringing in the ears, the harmony to which the universe was tuned. Plutarch's *Lives* and the plays of Aeschylus appealed to his admiration of the heroic, a strong transcendental characteristic. Jamblichus and Porphyry, from their neo-Platonic character, were required reading for all transcendentalists. Ovid Thoreau apparently read for the mythology and Vergil for his nature descriptions, for his representation of man's primitive closeness to the soil, and for his picture of the pastoral age, the Golden Age of the world.

The reading of the last two periods is self-explanatory, with the possible exceptions of Lucretius and the *Antigone* of Sophocles. Lucretius attempted in his poem, *De rerum natura,* the same thing that Thoreau was attempting, an explanation of the universe, and it was reasonable that Thoreau should be curious about it; but Lucretius' materialistic explanation could never interest a transcendentalist, and Thoreau found out of the first two hundred lines only two which interested him—a flaming description of the heroic Prometheus.[4]

9. Thoreau had read the *Antigone* at Harvard and had probably reread it by 1849. This would constitute a third reading.

1. The reader is reminded that such generalized information as the above may be made complete and specific by the use of the appendices.

2. *Writings,* I, 327; *The Week.*

3. *Ibid.,* VI, 102; letter to Emerson, August 7, 1843.

4. *Ibid.,* XIV, 312; journal of April 26, 1856.

The *Antigone*, however, cannot be so summarily dismissed. Although other classical works left much more specific quotation and reference in Thoreau's writing, the *Antigone* is probably responsible for one whole section of Thoreau's thought and public expression. From it must have come his concept of the divine law as superior to the civil law, of human right as greater than legal right. Its concepts lie behind the body of Thoreau's writing on government and politics; it is implicit in "Civil Disobedience" and in the articles on John Brown.

Other works yielded Thoreau minor images and symbols, figures, and myths that occur again and again in his writing: Homer's wood-chopper, Anacreon's cricket with its earth song; the *oestrus,* stinging to frenzy Io, men, and poets, and perhaps only a grub after all; Vergil's swelling buds and evening cottage smoke, the fable of Apollo and Admetus.

Much has been said of the influence of the classics on Thoreau's prose style. Latinity produces prolixity as often as it does compactness; involution as often as clarity. Thoreau's compactness and clarity are probably the result of his innumerable revisions; his Latinity is obvious, if at all, in his accuracy of word usage and perhaps in his neat and precise pronoun reference. But Thoreau could write in classical fashion when he chose to do so; he was a clever imitator of individual styles. He wrote four exquisite little Orphics, two versions of the poem "Fog," and two others, "Smoke" and "Haze."[5] They consist of the usual series of imaginative epithets addressed to some natural phenomenon but they have somewhat more body and solidity than the Greek Orphics. To these should be added the mad Orphic extravaganza to his moon-sister Diana,[6] the really lovely little Vergilian pastoral of the beautiful heifer[7] with all its fragmentary forerunners and reflections in the journal, and that delightful Catonian essay on "How to Catch a Pig."[8] Successful imitations indicate thorough familiarity with the models.

Although Thoreau believed that works should be read in the language in which they were written, he did not do all his classical reading in the original. He read some of the Greek texts in Latin translations; Aristotle in Greek and French. He read English translations also, although these were few.[9] He read a number of books which, although not classics, were written in the Latin language, such books as the Latin Linnaeus and the Latin Gray. It is quite obvious that his Latin is better than his Greek, but it is also obvious that his Greek is adequate, ade-

5. *Collected Poems of Henry Thoreau,* ed. Carl Bode (Chicago, Packard, 1943), pp. 27, 56, 59, 150.
6. *Writings,* VIII, 78; journal of 1850.
7. *Ibid.,* VIII, 67–8; journal of September, 1850.
8. *Ibid.,* XV, 260; journal of February 15, 1857.
9. Consult App. A for descriptions of classical books translated into other languages.

quate enough to enable him to compare information from different sources and to make cross references from one text to another.

Both the Latin and the Greek vocabularies are on the tip of his tongue, although Latin oftener than Greek. Once he forgets the Greek word for "waves" and has to substitute "sea" for it;[1] still he calls those same waves "social, multitudinous, ἀνήριθμον.[2] Running water reminds him of the Greek word ἔαρ;[3] the konchus tree makes him think of κόγχη,[4] and he starts speculating on a possible connection between the two.

We have spoken of this continual speculation on the origin, meaning, and relation of words in connection with the transcendental theory of language. Thoreau's philology seems fairly dependable. He allows his imagination to raise rather fanciful suggestions but he is careful not to make incorrect statements. He was quite aware of the pitfalls which philology offers to the amateur and once commented that the chief difference between an educated lecturer and one who had not had the advantages of formal education was that the educated man would "if the subject is the derivation of words . . . maintain a wise silence."[5]

Thoreau's translations from the classical languages into English show both his facility with the languages and the transcendental bias which colored all his study. The major translations, those of Aeschylus, Pindar, and Anacreon, belong to the literary period and partake of the nature of literary exercises. The *Prometheus Bound*[6] is very literally and ex-actly and unimaginatively rendered; word order is sometimes painfully preserved. There have been worse translations of the play, but Thoreau's does not rise above what it purported to be: a faithful and literal tran-script. The Pindar and Anacreon selections are more poetically done. Even though the Pindar was announced as a literal translation, there are passages of nature description and of heroism which are beautiful and stirring:

> With the javelin Phrastor struck the mark;
> And Eniceus cast the stone afar,
> Whirling his hand, above them all,
> And with applause it rushed
> Through a great tumult;
> And the lovely evening light
> Of the fair-faced moon shone on the scene.[7]

1. *Writings*, xii, 247; journal of May 8, 1854.
2. *Ibid.*, xvi, 127; journal of October 26, 1857.
3. *Ibid.*, ix, 363; journal of March 29, 1852.
4. *Ibid.*, iii, 120; "Chesuncook."
5. *Ibid.*, xix, 83; journal of January 8, 1860.
6. *Ibid.*, v, 337–75.
7. *Ibid.*, v, 378; Pindar, *Olympia* 10, 85–92.

Thoreau achieved here the economy and clarity of phrase of the Greek.

The Anacreon translations, taken as a whole, are the best of the published ones; Thoreau seems to have caught in them what he called their chief merit, "the lightness and yet security of their tread."[8] They are at the same time both literal and free, faithful to both the precision and the luxuriance of the originals.

Thoreau polished his translations in much the same way that he polished his English prose. We see the finished product in publication, but in a discarded manuscript fragment of the journal there exists Thoreau's work sheet for the translation of Ovid's version of the Phaëthon story, showing many revisions, deletions, insertions, substitutions.[9] In the manuscript Thoreau worked through the whole story; only a few lines of it appeared in print.[1]

But the printed translations were meant for publication, and they necessarily answer with varying degrees of excellence certain orthodox standards of accuracy and fidelity to source. It is in the fragmentary translations scattered throughout Thoreau's works that we see what his own standards of translation were. The snowflake simile from the *Iliad* is an excellent illustration. As most readers will recall, Homer is comparing the battle of the Achaeans and the Trojans to a snowstorm. The passage runs like this:

And as flakes of snow fall thick on a winter's day, when the counselor Zeus rouses himself to snow, revealing these arrows to men, and he lulls the winds, and showers down the flakes steadily until he has covered the tops of the high mountains and the headlands, and the meadows and the fertile fields of man; yes, and the harbors and the shores of the gray sea, too, though the beating waves wash it away, but all other things are clothed with the snow when the fury of Zeus drives it on; so from both sides the stones flew thick, both on the Trojans and from the Trojans upon the Achaeans, as they hurled them at each other, and the tumult rose up over the wall.[2]

This is what Thoreau does with it:

The snowflakes fall thick and fast on a winter's day. The winds are lulled, and the snow falls incessant, covering the tops of the mountains, and the hills, and the plains where the lotus tree grows, and the cultivated fields. And they are falling by the inlets and shores of the foaming sea, but are silently dissolved by the waves.[3]

It is beautiful poetry, reminiscent both of Alcman's "Night" and of Goethe's "Night Song," both of which Thoreau may quite possibly have

8. *Writings*, I, 239; *The Week*.
9. *Huntington Journal Fragments (HM13182)*.
1. *Writings*, VIII, 144–5; journal of 1851.
2. Homer, *Iliad*, XII, 278–89.
3. *Writings*, VII, 61; journal of October 24, 1838; also III, 181–2, "A Winter Walk."

known.[4] But the interesting thing about it is that Thoreau has taken from the original only what spoke to him. He has stripped the passage of circumstance, all that was local and temporal and particular, and has kept only the universal. A battle between the Achaeans and the Trojans is a trivial matter, but the blanketing peace of the snow is an eternal reality.

When Thoreau read and translated for himself, he was not at all concerned with fidelity to the original; he was not concerned with verb tenses or with completeness of content. As he omitted, so he patched, putting together into one context widely separated lines.[5] He wanted the heart of the matter. And to a transcendentalist the heart of the matter was what answered to a man's individual genius. The prophet from the past spoke his revelation, but each man weighed the revelation in his own heart and accepted that which was for him. A very slight extension of this practice permits a man to read his own meaning into another's words. Thoreau once remarked that he suspected that the Greeks were commonly innocent of the meanings attributed to them;[6] he made a much more definite statement to that effect about the Orientals. Speaking of the Rig Veda, he said that it meant "more or less as the reader is more or less alert and imaginative," and added, ". . . I am sometimes inclined to doubt if the translator has not made something out of nothing, —whether a real idea or sentiment has been thus transmitted to us from so primitive a period." But he considered the matter quite unimportant, "for I do not the least care where I get my ideas, or what suggests them."[7]

It was a philosophy like this which enabled him not only to select from the classics whatever he wanted but even to read into the classics ideas which were strictly his own. Of Anacreon's poems he made the remarkable statement that "they are not gross, as has been presumed, but always elevated above the sensual."[8] The statement is possibly half true, depending upon the definition of "sensual"; certainly their exquisite expression elevates them above the sensual in the most unfavorable meaning of the word, but just as certainly their whole basis is sensual in any meaning of the word, and only a very innocent mind could deny it.

Horace and Persius Thoreau deliberately mistranslated, knowing

4. Thoreau owned two books (App. A, Nos. 37, 40) which included the poems of Alcman. He did not mention Alcman or quote from him. He also read extensively in Goethe, but he made no mention of this lyric.

5. See App. B, "Horace," for an example of this. See his treatment of the last two chapters of Tacitus' *Agricola* in "After the Death of John Brown," *Writings,* IV, 452–4, as an example of taking liberties with classical text.

6. *Writings,* XVI, 227; journal of December 27, 1857.

7. *Ibid.,* XIV, 135; journal of January 24, 1856.

8. *Ibid.,* I, 240; *The Week.*

quite well that the lines meant one thing as Horace and Persius wrote them but finding a second meaning more acceptable to himself.[9]

Certainly Thoreau was a classicist; he was competent in language and grammar; his reading was wide; his translation was dependable according to his purpose. But he was not a classicist for the sake of classicism. He was a classicist, just as he was a naturalist or a hermit or a writer, only because and as far as his classicism furthered his search for reality. It was only as the classics were related to the quest that they had meaning and value for Thoreau.

9. This is discussed and illustrated in Chap. II.

II

Embarkation

"To tell the truth, I saw an advertisement for able-bodied seamen, when I was a boy, sauntering in my native port, and as soon as I came of age I embarked."

IT would be interesting to know at what age Thoreau read the advertisement and exactly what form it took. Edward Emerson recalls a story told by Thoreau's mother that when Henry was so small a boy as to be sleeping in a trundle bed she found him wide awake late one night and asked the reason. Thoreau answered, "Mother, I have been looking through the stars to see if I couldn't find God behind them."[1] This is a delightful story in view of the fact that Thoreau did spend his life doing very nearly that; but such statements have been made by hundreds of little boys who did not grow up to be Thoreaus, and it would be nonsense to suggest seriously that Thoreau had at that time read his advertisement. Several later statements, however, do seem to suggest that the advertisement may have been printed in the form of a book. In *Walden* Thoreau reflects that many a man has dated a new era in his life from the reading of a book;[2] and in the journal of 1838 he is impressed by the similarity of his circumstances to those of Zeno, a man "bred a merchant," who read a book one day and became a philosopher.[3]

Thoreau's borrowings from the Harvard library during his college days constitute the first record we have of voluntary reading on his part.[4] Some of the titles furnish an opportunity for speculation: Burgh's *The Dignity of Human Nature, or a brief account of the certain and established means for attaining the true end of our existence;* Tucker's *The Light of Nature Pursued;* Burke's *A Philosophical Enquiry into the Origin of our Ideas of the Sublime and Beautiful;* and of a more practical than theoretical character, Schlegel's *Lectures on the History of Literature* and Bailey's *Essays on the Formation and Publication of Opinions and on Other Subjects.* Of these, Burgh seems at first glance most likely

1. Edward W. Emerson, *Henry Thoreau as Remembered by a Young Friend* (Boston and New York, Houghton Mifflin, 1917), pp. 14–15.
2. *Writings*, II, 120.
3. *Ibid.*, VII, 26–7; journal of February 7, 1838.
4. Kenneth Cameron has published a list of Thoreau's withdrawals from the Harvard College library in his *Emerson, the Essayist* (Raleigh, North Carolina, The Thistle Press, 1945), II, 191–208. I have used his identifications for the books mentioned here.

to have been the advertisement, since he was favorite reading in the Thoreau household[5] and since Alcott said in his journal that of all the books which he read as a youth Burgh's *Dignity* and Bunyan's *Pilgrim's Progress* did more than any others to shape the course of his life.[6] Burgh, however, is in the eighteenth-century tradition of conventionality, conformity, prudence, decorum, and thrift, and it seems preposterous that the book could have influenced either Alcott's or Thoreau's life in any other way than as a teetotaler father often produces a drunkard son! Thoreau himself referred to it with a kind of amused tolerance.[7] And Tucker's *Light of Nature,* for all its suggestive title, is also eighteenth century in character. If there was any one book which determined Thoreau's life, it is still undiscovered.

All the books, however, are interesting indications of an early philosophical and literary bias and seem germinal to some of Thoreau's later interests. Germinal, certainly, of his antiquarian obsession was his reading in four installments of Rollin's eight-volume *Ancient History,* a book which he recommended to his sister Helen several years later for its "exploits of the brave."[8] It covered, as its long title announced, the history of the Egyptians, Carthaginians, Assyrians, Babylonians, Medes, Persians, Macedonians, and Greeks. Thoreau supplemented this with Goldsmith's *History of Rome* and rounded out his ancient history with Anville's *A Complete Body of Ancient Geography.*

The classics are represented in these early library borrowings, but they seem in most cases simply auxiliary to the college course of study, and in others they suggest even that Thoreau had mislaid his textbook and had to make temporary provision for another! Cleveland's *Epitome of Grecian Antiquities,* Fisk's *Greek Exercises,* and Euripides' *Alcestis* were all school texts. The two Greek dictionaries and Harwood's *Grecian Antiquities*[9] seem obviously supplementary. In fact, Thoreau went through the regular classical course at Harvard[1]—two years of Latin and three years of Greek grammar; two years of the study of Greek and Roman antiquities; the reading in Greek of the crown orations of Aeschines and Demosthenes, Xenophon's *Anabasis,* Sophocles' three

5. *Writings,* VI, 99; letter to Thoreau's mother, August 6, 1843.
6. *The Journals of Bronson Alcott,* ed. Odell Shepard, p. 459; journal of June 16, 1875.
7. *Writings,* VI, 99; letter to Thoreau's mother, August 6, 1843.
8. *Ibid.,* VI, 31; letter to Helen, January 23, 1840. At this time Thoreau was making a collection of thoughts on bravery for such articles as "The Qualities of the Recruit" and "The Service."
9. See App. A, Nos. 11, 14, 19–22 for descriptions of these books.
1. Before he reached Harvard he had read all of Vergil, Cicero's *Select Orations,* and a Greek anthology containing mostly prose selections, but a few pages from the *Iliad.* He had studied Adam's *Latin Grammar* and Buttman's *Greek Grammar* and may possibly have read some of Sallust and of the Greek Testament. See App. A, Nos. 1–5 and Supplement to App. A, Nos. 1–3. For the Harvard texts here mentioned see App. A, Nos. 6–18, 21, and Supplement to App. A, Nos. 4–7.

Theban plays,[2] and Euripides' *Alcestis*,[3] and in Latin of Horace's *Odes, Satires,* and *Epistles,* selections from Livy, the *Medea* of Seneca, Cicero's *De claris oratoribus* and *De officiis,* and Juvenal's properly expurgated *Satires*—without showing any special interest until he reached his junior year and Homer. Then we find him supplementing Felton's *Iliad,* which was used at Harvard, with the scholarly Heyne edition, reading Hobbes' seventeenth-century English translation of the *Iliad* and the *Odyssey,* and expressing his enthusiasm over Homer to a friend.[4]

His enthusiasm persisted beyond the end of the course, for Thoreau's study of the *Iliad* and his classical studies at Harvard ended with his junior year;[5] but in his senior year he withdrew from the library, read, and wrote a review of Henry Nelson Coleridge's little book, *Introductions to the Study of the Greek Classic Poets.*[6] Several ideas from this book appear later in Thoreau's thought: a distinction between the literatures of northern and southern races, a strong admiration for Aeschylus,[7] much discussion of Greek mythology, and even certain favorite passages from Homer, among them the famous snowflake simile and the picture of Apollo coming νυκτὶ ἐοικώς upon the Greeks.[8]

There are a few classical references in his college themes, corresponding usually to his required current reading in the classics.[9] They seem

2. The *Oedipus Tyrannus, Oedipus Colonus,* and *Antigone.* See App. C for Thoreau's references to these.

3. The *Alcestis* which Thoreau withdrew from the Harvard College library was bound with the *Ion.* It is not necessary to assume, however, even considering Thoreau's interest in the *oestrus* element of the Io story, that he read the *Ion.* His interest may have come from Aeschylus' *Prometheus,* from history, mythology, or philology generally, from his natural history reading in Kirby and Spence, or, as internal evidence of style would seem to indicate, from Ovid.

4. F. B. Sanborn, *The Life of Henry David Thoreau* (Boston and New York, Houghton Mifflin, 1917), pp. 59, 63; letter to Rice, August 5, 1836.

5. I do not understand the prevalence of what seems to me certainly a rumor that Jones Very was Thoreau's Greek tutor at Harvard. Jones Very was graduated in 1836 and named Greek tutor for 1837, Thoreau's senior year, when Thoreau was no longer studying Greek. He may, of course, have known Jones Very, but even the exaggerating Sanborn will say no more than that.

6. See App. A, No. 25. The review is No. 7 of a group of exercises in *HM934.* It is dated October 1, 1836.

7. Thoreau's reference to this distinction in a section of comment on Aeschylus (*Writings,* VII, 116; journal of January 29, 1840) would suggest that the two were associated in his mind and possibly came from the same source.

8. Homer, *Iliad* xii, 278–85; Coleridge, pp. 102–3; *Writings,* VII, 61, and Homer, *Iliad* i, 47; Coleridge, p. 14; *Writings,* VII, 31. These similes are very popular ones.

9. Sanborn, *The Life of Henry David Thoreau,* pp. 54–189, has printed and discussed twenty-seven college essays. *HM934* contains manuscript of seven including Nos. 1, 2, 3, 4, 12, and 21 in Sanborn and the Coleridge review mentioned above. I list classical quotation in the essays:

  a. "The Literary Life" (Sanborn, pp. 85–7, theme 7). Horace, *Serm.* ii, 2, 77. Thoreau was currently reading Horace.

  b. "Characteristics of Milton's Poesy" (Sanborn, pp. 93–7, theme 9). One English quotation attributed to Cicero, whose *De claris oratoribus* and *De officiis* Thoreau was reading.

to be decorative in the popular style of the period and to have little significance. Probably the themes of any Harvard student of the same period would yield an equal amount of classical tone and color.[1]

There are more significant traces of classicism, however, in the manuscript notebook known as the *Index Rerum* which Thoreau began in his college years. One is a review of Adam Ferguson's *History of the Progress and Termination of the Roman Empire*.[2] Thoreau's interest in the book was not historical; the review took the shape of a list of original sources from which Roman history could be studied; that is, a comprehensive outline of Latin literature. Throughout his life, whenever Thoreau found an area of knowledge which interested him, he constructed an outline for a study guide. He did not always follow his outlines, nor did he follow this one, but its existence is witness to the fact that he once intended to read the body of Latin literature.

Another item in the *Index Rerum,* the Latin inscription for the cenotaph of the Indian chief,[3] has been publicized because of its entertainment value, but it is very much the kind of thing any bright youngster is likely to try his hand on. In the nineteenth century an Indian cenotaph seemed an appropriate subject for experiment; in the twentieth century young Latin students translate popular songs. In this century, however, they do not achieve passive periphrastic constructions in their nonsense!

There is one other evidence of classical interest in the scanty record of these early years.[4] It appears that before Thoreau was graduated from Harvard he acquired some ten classical books which were not textbooks: American Delphine editions of Juvenal and Persius and of the *Metamorphoses* of Ovid; a Zeunii edition of Horace which he used in later years in preference to the Gould classroom edition; Dryden's

---

c. "Fate Among the Ancients" (Sanborn, pp. 175-7, theme 24). This contains a discussion of the Greek concept of fate, an English quotation from Plato, and one in Latin from Cicero's *De divinatione* (i, 122) followed by the English translation. These are probably second hand, since they do not come within the scope of Thoreau's classical reading as we know it.

d. "Titus Pomponius Atticus as an Example" (Sanborn, pp. 183-5, theme 27). There are two English quotations and one Latin from Nepos' *Lives*. The English quotation furnishes a good example of Thoreau's habit of combining widely separated sentences into what seems to be a consecutive series. For a description of the Nepos see App. A, No. 26.

1. Such classicism was a part of the paraphernalia of conscious culture in the first half of the nineteenth century. Thoreau was actually less infected by it than were Channing, Emerson, and Alcott, all of whom confessed their own inadequacies as classical scholars.

2. *Index Rerum* (HM945), pp. 29ᵛ–31ᵛ.

3. *Ibid.,* p. 32ʳ. Sanborn has made an inaccurate transcription of this (*The Life of Henry David Thoreau,* p. 186). I have not seen it printed correctly.

4. The Decius-Cato dialogue in Greek, written for a Harvard exhibition exercise in 1835, may indicate proficiency, but scarcely any voluntary interest, in the classics.

translations of Vergil and the cheap Langhorne translation of Plutarch's *Lives;* Xenophon's *Cyropaedia* in Greek and Latin and Curtius' *History of Alexander the Great;* Ainsworth's abridged Latin dictionary, Pickering's new Greek-English lexicon, and Lemprière's *Classical Dictionary.*[5] How he acquired them it is impossible to say; they might conceivably have been gifts, but the historical and the philological books would seem to be Thoreau's own selection. If a student as poor as Thoreau actually bought ten nonrequired classical books during his college career, that would be evidence of a real love of the classics.

But whether we believe that Thoreau found anything more in the classics during his school days than most young people do—the satisfaction of a romantic curiosity—there are very definite indications in the record of these years that Thoreau knew what the purpose of his life was to be. As early as 1835 he copied into a notebook comments of Longfellow on poets and poetry: the theory that poetry originated in the pastoral scenes of the Golden Age, the idea that poetry is for instruction as well as for pleasure and that it serves as a stimulus to noble action, the belief that the poet finds his greatest inspiration in nature.[6] In the essay, "The Literary Life," he emphasized the solitary quality of that life,[7] and in a book review of Howitt's *The Book of the Seasons* he copied a quotation from Schlegel in which the correlation was made between the poet's solitude and his communion with nature: "It is for the purpose . . . of holding mysterious converse with the soul of nature, that every great poet is a lover of solitude." [8]

In another essay, "The Story-Telling Faculty," he offered the writer a second source of inspiration and information: ". . . the page of History is never closed, the Castalian Spring is never dry. The volume of Nature is ever open; the story of the world never ceases to interest."[9] History and poetry reveal the story of the universe vertically through time in the concentrated experience of humanity. Nature and the world reveal the same story horizontally through space in the repeated forms and patterns of life.

Of all the college writing the most prophetic, perhaps, was a theme on journal-keeping. In this Thoreau gave two reasons for keeping a journal: first, to sift experience into truth and second, to express the result. Keeping a journal is like striking a daily balance, casting out the

5. For description of these books see App. A, Nos. 27–34, and Supplement to App. A, Nos. 8–9.

6. I have seen photostat of this through the courtesy of the late Mr. H. W. L. Dana of Cambridge, Massachusetts.

7. He gave Horace as an example of a poet who lived a solitary life! Later he put Chaucer in the same category.

8. *Index Rerum* (HM945), p. 22ᵛ. It was soon after this that Thoreau withdrew Schlegel's *Lectures on the History of Literature* from the Harvard College library. It was characteristic of Thoreau to go from secondary to primary reading in an author.

9. Sanborn, *The Life of Henry David Thoreau,* p. 119, theme 13.

false coin and adding up the gains. A journal properly kept gives us the means of improving ourselves "by reflection, by making a habit of thinking, and by giving our thought form and expression."[1] A record of what we have done keeps us from futile repetition. Thoreau expressed in this theme also the centrality of the individual's experience, urging the study of self as the principal means to knowledge, and the study of others and of books mainly "to detect any errors."

The title of the theme is as interesting and almost as inclusive as its content: "Of Keeping a private Journal or Record of our Thoughts, Feelings, Studies, and daily Experience,—containing abstracts of Books, and the Opinions We formed of them on first reading them." Thoreau eventually made a division of the material which he here suggests as content for a journal, reserving the journal for his daily experiences, thoughts, and feelings and transferring his reading to his commonplace books, so that we follow the quest through the journal but are sometimes forced to consult the commonplace books to discover what tools he is using. In neither place do we find much factual biography,[2] for this did not come under Thoreau's definition of truth. Indeed, Thoreau tried to apply the journal standard of reporting to his letters, restricting himself either to the "emotions of the soul" or to silence, an attitude that annoyed his sister Helen.[3] It sometimes annoys us too in the journal, for we have continually to make our own correlation between the events of his physical life and the progress of his quest.

Thoreau was graduated from Harvard on August 16, 1837; he felt himself at last a free agent. "You know we have hardly done our own deeds, thought our own thoughts, or lived our own lives hitherto," he wrote to Helen in the fall of that year.[4] Outwardly his life was not remarkable in the eight years between Harvard and Walden; he taught school, worked for Emerson, tutored, wrote a few articles for publication, made pencils. But all the time he was engaged in his own private search; studying himself, the world, and his books, waiting for the revelation, sifting in his journal the intimations which came to him.

He wasted no time in embarking. Three days after commencement he summarized and recorded his approval of the poet-prophet concept by quoting in his commonplace book part of the closing passage of Sidney's *Defense of Poesy*.[5] This selection not only defined the poet

1. *Ibid.*, pp. 73–4, theme 4. Notice how close the quotation is to Sanborn's statement that the business of Thoreau's life was observation, writing, and reading. Thoreau, however, indicates that these are means rather than ends.

2. This statement does not hold true for the late journals.

3. *Writings*, VI, 13; letter to Helen, October 27, 1837: ". . . letter-writing too often degenerates into a communicating of facts, and not of truths. . . . What are the convulsions of a planet, compared with the emotions of the soul?" See also *ibid.*, VI, 32; letter to Helen, June 13, 1840.

4. *Ibid.*, VI, 12; letter to Helen, October 27, 1837.

5. *College Note-Book (MA. 594)*, p. 29ʳ.

but offered an explanation of the truth which the poet was to utter, identifying it as all knowledge in the form of myth, and it recommended the reading of Vergil for the making of an "honest man" and the reading of Homer and Hesiod for the discovery of the mythological truth.

On October 22 Thoreau began his journal. The journal of these early years is particularly valuable for our purposes, consisting as it does not of the original entries but of transcripts made by Thoreau at a later time. It is labeled "Gleanings or What Time has not Reaped of my Journal." The editors of the journals have apparently taken this to mean what was left of the journal after material had been extracted for publication, but since much of the material still remaining appears once or more times in published form, the title seems rather to mean what time has not proved trivial or false; that is, what Thoreau has found true over a period of years. In so concentrated a record—360 printed pages for the years 1837–42—every entry seems important.[6]

In the first entry Thoreau demanded the solitude essential for the life of a poet. In the third and fourth entries he set forth his concept of the poet, using Goethe's description from *Torquato Tasso*.

> He seems to avoid—even to flee from us,—
> To seek something which we know not,
> And perhaps he himself after all knows not.
>
> His eye hardly rests upon the earth;
> His ear hears the one-clang of nature;
> What history records,—what life gives,—
> Directly and gladly his genius takes it up :[7]

In these seven lines are contained the ideas of the poet's solitary life, his quest for the unnamable, and his discernment of the essential unity of all things, recorded both in the history of the past and in the variety of the present.

Thoreau, too, was looking for that central unity; studying himself, the vapors and shadows that clouded the soul; observing nature, trying little, tentative descriptions of fragmentary views, careful even this early to avoid the mechanical accumulation of fact;[8] reading his books in the hope that the past might reveal the secret. He counseled himself to patience, resolving to "float with the current"; he remarked the shy and evanescent character of truth; but he must' have expected fairly

6. In so condensed a record the reader will have no difficulty locating material of a summary or generalized nature or that approximately located by comment in the text. I shall document only quotation and specific reference essential for proof or illustration.

7. *Writings*, VII, 4; journal of October 25, 26, 1837.

8. *Ibid.*, VII, 18; journal of December 16, 1837, "Facts."

quick results, for less than two months after he embarked upon the quest he wrote regretfully, "I yet lack discernment to distinguish the whole lesson of today; but it is not lost,—it will come to me at last. My desire is to know *what* I have lived, that I may know *how* to live henceforth."[9]

Out of the scattered observations some certainties emerge. Whether or not he was following Sidney's exhortation, Thoreau began in November to reread Vergil's *Eclogues,* the pastoral poetry of the Golden Age.[1] He was pleased to find there a reassuring and authoritative confirmation of his theory of the eternal sameness of things. "I would read Virgil," he said, "if only that I might be reminded of the identity of human nature in all ages. . . . It was the same world, and the same men inhabited it."[2] The lines he quoted, however, were from the world and nature rather than from men and human nature: the valleys echoing to the stars, the buds swelling on the branches, the apples scattered beneath the trees. Only in the shepherd's stabling of his flocks at night do we find any mention of man.

The next substantiation of the essential identity of all things came from the world of nature also, but from Thoreau's world rather than Vergil's, from observation rather than reading. Studying the patterns of hoar frost and concluding that crystallization and vegetation obeyed one law, he wondered whether the leaf might not be the basic pattern of things.[3] It was not a very tenable idea and he seemed to abandon it reluctantly a few days later: "I tried to fancy that there was a disposition in these crystallizations to take the forms of the contiguous foliage."[4] But he never completely abandoned it; it appears in "The Natural History of Massachusetts," here and there throughout the journals, and in elaborated form and with philological adornment in the lobe-lip-leaf fantasy of *Walden.*[5]

During this year Thoreau made a minor investigation of the transcendental theory of language, finding beneath the words "digit," "span," and "fathom" the natural and spiritual facts of which they were the symbols.[6] In addition, he gave expression to two ideas which were to become almost obsessions with him and which were eventually to be related to each other. One was the idea of the musical harmony to be

9. *Ibid.,* VII, 9; journal of November 12, 1837.

1. The quotations are from *Eclogues* 6 and 7. Whether he read more at this time is not known. For quotations see App. B, "Vergil." For description of text see App. A, No. 35.

2. *Writings,* VII, 12; journal of November 20, 1837.

3. *Ibid.,* VII, 14; journal of November 28, 1837.

4. *Ibid.,* VII, 22; journal of December 23, 1837.

5. See also Sanborn, *The First and Last Journeys of Thoreau* (Boston, The Bibliophile Society, 1905), I, 78–9. This statement comes from the *Huntington Journal Fragments* (*HM13182*) of the early 1840's.

6. *Writings,* VII, 15; journal of December 10, 1837.

found in the sounds of nature;[7] the other was the story of the golden grasshopper of the Athenians, symbol of their earth-born origin.[8] It became for Thoreau a symbol of man's unity with the earth, of continuity and immortality. He managed later to transfer these connotations from the grasshopper to the cricket, and the chirping of the cricket became for him earth song, the most delightful of nature's harmonies, the very essence of music.[9]

He closed the year on a note of patience and hope. In a few months he had checked two theories and found them true. He had found two valuable and suggestive symbols, the leaf and the grasshopper. He had felt faintly the rhythm and harmony of the universe. He was picking up the *disjecta membra* of truth and was not discouraged.[1]

The first entries of 1838 abounded in contentment. Thoreau rejoiced in his ability to make his own future and happiness. He reflected that beauty was everywhere and always the same, in Rome or in Concord. His mind kept turning toward the classics; he looked for new paths to explore. It seems a little pitiful that he should have been driven to such provender as Lemprière's *Classical Dictionary,* but he found there a man worthy of his admiration—Zeno the stoic.[2] Zeno, he was pleased to discover, stood in precisely the same relation to the world that he did, that of the solitary seeker who every evening, like a good journal keeper, sat down to review the events of the day. On the data in the *Classical Dictionary* Thoreau could not greatly expand his study of Zeno, but still he turned toward the classics. "In imagination," he said, "I hie me to Greece as to enchanted ground."[3] An analysis of the paragraph which follows this statement explains the enchantment; it was the embalmed, remote, unchanging quality of ancient Greece which appealed to him. Always Thoreau was to find distance, faintness, remoteness a help to perception whether of sound or view or fact or experience. The immediate world was a sprawling subject for a young student to handle; one hardly knew where to lay hold on it. But there, crystallized in time, lay the Golden Age of the world, and perhaps following another of Sidney's suggestions "that it pleased the heavenly deity by Hesiod and Homer, under the veil of fables, to give us all knowledge," he began to reread the *Iliad.*

7. *Ibid.,* VII, 12; journal of November 18, 1837, "Harmony."

8. *Ibid.,* VII, 19; journal of December 18, 1837, "Immortality Post."

9. *Ibid.,* VII, 57; journal of August 27, 1838, "Crickets." See also *ibid.,* VIII, 306; journal of July 14, 1851, for an excellent expression of a frequently repeated idea.

1. *Ibid.,* VII, 24; journal of December 31, 1837. The phrase comes from the *Medea.* It is worth while to read carefully the first and last entries to each year's journal. In them, or in some entry toward the beginning and end, Thoreau often gives a kind of preview of intention or summary of thought.

2. *Writings,* VII, 26–7; journal of February 7, 1838. It was a book of Xenophon's that made Zeno a philosopher. Thoreau had already read some of Xenophon's history; we shall soon find him trying his philosophical writing. For a description of Lemprière see App. A, No. 34.

3. *Writings,* VII, 29; journal of February 16, 1838.

He did not finish it that year,[4] but he found in it the same thing that he had found in Vergil's *Eclogues,* the continuity and permanence of certain patterns. "Three thousand years and the world so little changed!" was his first comment. The fire-eyed Agamemnon reminded him of equally fiery-eyed declaimers at town meetings and elections. He found a female Nestor "of the old school" among his mother's Sunday visitors.[5] He found in Homer also what Sidney had promised: that mythology which contained all knowledge. Of Pallas Athene's coming from Heaven to allay Achilles' wrath, he questioned, "Men may dispute about the fact whether a goddess did actually come down from heaven, calling it a poet's fancy, but was it not, considering the stuff that gods are made of, a very truth?"[6] Many a wrathful man's good genius has counseled him to peace.

The simplicity of the *Iliad* made a strong appeal to him, both the simplicity of the expression, which was the mark of the true poet,[7] and the simplicity of the life pictured in the poem—the woodcutter spreading his morning meal,[8] Nestor's simple repast after the rescue of Machaon. His satisfaction in this simplicity had a deeper source than the obvious. To Thoreau simplicity and antiquity were almost synonymous; both involved a reduction to first things. As he had a kind of feeling that he might get down to first things in the present by reducing life to an extreme simplicity, so he felt that he might get back to first things in the past if he could get far enough back. Even Homer was not far enough. In an original poem called "Walden," written in June of this year, he expressed his desire to go back behind time and history.

> O! tell me what the winds have writ for the last thousand years
> On the blue vault that spans thy flood,
> Or sun transferred and delicately reprinted
> For thy own private reading. Somewhat
> Within these latter days I've read,
> But surely there was much that would have thrilled the Soul,
> Which human eye saw not.
> I would give much to read that first bright page,
> Wet from a virgin press, when Eurus, Boreas,
> And the host of airy quill-drivers
> First dipped their pens in mist.[9]

4. The spring quotations are from Bk. I of the *Iliad,* the fall quotations from Bks. XI and XII. Summer journal entries are few. Henry wrote to his brother John (*Writings,* VI, 23; July 8, 1838) that he was reading Greek, and since no indication of any other classical reading appears he was probably reading the *Iliad.* For passages quoted see App. B, "Homer."

5. *Writings,* VII, 31; journal of March 3, 4, 1838.

6. *Ibid.,* VII, 33; journal of March 5, 1838.

7. *Ibid.,* VII, 56; journal of August 26, 1838, "Homer," and VII, 59; journal of September 7, 1838, "Homer."

8. The woodcutter was, like the golden grasshopper, another of Thoreau's idealizations and reappears innumerable times in the *Writings.*

9. *Writings,* VII, 50–1; June 3, 1838.

Perhaps the influence of the classroom and the library was giving way to that of the Concord countryside. In March he had been dissatisfied with his journal-keeping and his slowness of accomplishment;[1] in the summer, teaching school, he read a little in Greek and English, wrote poetry in the conventional sense of the word, and took long afternoon walks. In late summer he recorded mystic experience.

If with closed ears and eyes I consult consciousness for a moment, immediately are all walls and barriers dissipated, earth rolls from under me, and I float, by the impetus derived from the earth and the system, a subjective, heavily laden thought, in the midst of an unknown and infinite sea, or else heave and swell like a vast ocean of thought, without rock or headland, where are all riddles solved, all straight lines making there their two ends to meet, eternity and space gambolling familiarly through my depths. I am from the beginning, knowing no end, no aim. No sun illumines me, for I dissolve all lesser lights in my own intenser and steadier light. I am a restful kernel in the magazine of the universe.[2]

Whatever he found would be his own discovery.

Men are constantly dinging in my ears their fair theories and plausible solutions of the universe, but ever there is no help, and I return again to my shoreless, islandless ocean, and fathom unceasingly for a bottom that will hold an anchor, that it may not drag.[3]

He became increasingly perceptive toward sound. The whisper of the woods, the sounds of evening revelry, the chant of the cricket, the song of birds, the peeping of frogs, the crowing of the cock were all strains of sphere music.[4] His soul responded. "The human soul is a silent harp in God's quire, whose strings need only to be swept by the divine breath to chime in with the harmonies of creation."[5]

The sentiments of the oldest books were music too, a part of the great harmony, "a strain of music wafted down to us on the breeze of time, through the aisles of innumerable ages."[6] The cricket's song and Homer's might easily be one. "It matters not whether these strains originate there in the grass or float thitherward like atoms of light from the minstrel days of Greece."[7] Nature and the poet, the world and history proclaimed the same message.

The summation of his year's experience with Homer, with nature, and within himself came in the essay "Sound and Silence" written in the last half of December. He defined sounds as exquisite but imperfect

---

1. *Ibid.*, VII, 34–5; journal of March 5, 6, 1838.
2. *Ibid.*, VII, 53–4; journal of August 13, 1838.
3. *Ibid.*, VII, 54; journal of August 13, 1838.
4. *Ibid.*, VII, 51–2; July 8, 1838, "Cliffs"; *ibid.*, VII, 57, 58, 55.
5. *Ibid.*, VII, 53; journal of August 10, 1838.
6. *Ibid.*, VII, 55; journal of August 22, 1838.
7. *Ibid.*, VII, 61; journal of October 24, 1838.

approximations of the greatest of all harmonies, silence. He affirmed that "the Grecian, or *silent* and melodious, Era, is ever sounding on the ears of men." He praised a good book as the "plectrum with which our silent lyres are struck."[8]

Toward the close of the year Thoreau took a tentative step into a new field of classical literature, one closely associated with his sensitivity to sound and with his fondness for the story of the golden grasshopper. He read and translated Anacreon's "Ode to the Cicada," and he liked its music well enough to continue with the "Return of Spring" and "Cupid Wounded."[9] He would read and translate many more within the next few years.

It must have been a good year, a rounded and satisfactory year, but the young poet was forced to admit at the end of it that he could not interpret the silence.

It were vain for me to interpret the Silence. She cannot be done into English. For six thousand years have men translated her, with what fidelity belonged to each; still she is little better than a sealed book. A man may run on confidently for a time, thinking he has her under his thumb, and shall one day exhaust her, but he too must at last be silent, and men remark only how brave a beginning he made; for, when he at length dives into her, so vast is the disproportion of the told to the untold that the former will seem but the bubble on the surface where he disappeared.[1]

The discovery of truth was not so easy as it once seemed. "Nevertheless will we go on, like those Chinese cliff swallows, feathering our nests with the froth, so they may one day be bread of life to such as dwell by the seashore."[2]

In the next two years the tone of the journal changed. It did not show the steady confidence, the consistent growth, of 1838. It showed, indeed, a slight uncertainty and variation, not so much the result of despondency or disillusion as of new and conflicting interests. In 1838 Thoreau had begun to live somewhat less as an individual and more as a member of society. He had been admitted to close association with Emerson; he had given his first Lyceum lecture—on "Society" incidentally; he had made a trip to Maine to look for a school; he had taught

8. *Ibid.*, VII, 68; "Sound and Silence."

9. *Ibid.*, VII, 66, 69–70. The first two odes also appear in *ibid.*, V, 108–10, and in the *Dial*, III, No. 3 (July, 1842), 23–4. "Cupid Wounded" appears among other selections from Anacreon in the *Dial*, III, No. 4 (April, 1843), 484–90. This article is also printed in *Writings*, I, 238–44. These are Thoreau's first translations of any length with the exception of the snowflake simile already mentioned. I do not know where Thoreau read these Anacreontics, for he had not yet acquired the *Minor Greek Poets*. I suspect that the source was the *Graeca Minora*, a standard academy text until 1826 and generally available. It should perhaps be added that the scholarship of Thoreau's time attributed to Anacreon a number of poems since judged to be merely imitations.

1. *Writings*, VII, 68–9; December, 1838, "Sound and Silence."

2. *Ibid.*

briefly in the town school before establishing his own. In 1839 his active participation in affairs of the world increased. With his brother John he was teaching a successful school. With John he took the trip to be commemorated in *The Week;*[3] and still in company with John he fell in love![4] By 1840 he found himself an accepted member of a little band of intellectuals. In May of that year he met with the group at Emerson's to· discuss "The Inspiration of the Prophet and Bard, the Nature of Poetry and the Causes of the Sterility of the Poetic Inspiration in our own Age and Country." In July the first issue of the transcendental organ, the *Dial,* appeared, and Thoreau had an article in it.[5] He dwelt not so exclusively in the spirit now and more in Concord.

In the writing of these years Thoreau had an eye steadily on publication. He continued to develop and define his criticism of poetry, later to be incorporated into the lecture and *Dial* essay, "Homer. Ossian. Chaucer."[6] He worked on the classical translations which would eventually find their way into the *Dial.* And he began a collection of lecture and essay notes on two new subjects, "Friendship" and "Bravery." Both subjects were indicative of his growing relationship to the world of men. Into "Friendship" went the perplexities of his adjustment to other human beings and probably, in disguised form, the perplexities of his affair with Ellen Sewall. Into "Bravery" went his high hopes for himself; the qualities which the wise man, the virtuous man, the courageous man, the philosopher, should exhibit in his life in the world.[7]

Most of the reading of the period contributed in some way or other to this picture of the brave man. If Thoreau read in the classics in the spring and summer of 1839, he did not record it; but in November he was reading Aeschylus' *Prometheus Bound*[8] and by January of the

---

3. Although this trip was taken in 1839, the manuscript for the book was largely prepared at Walden (1845–47) and the book was not published until 1849. An examination of the passages in the book dealing with Thoreau's classical interests and his own development shows that most of these were insertions of the Walden period. They will be discussed in the next chapter.

4. For recent discussions of this see Henry Seidel Canby, *Thoreau* (Boston, Houghton Mifflin, 1939), pp. 111–26, and Joseph Wood Krutch, *Thoreau* (New York, William Sloane Associates, 1948), pp. 30–4.

5. "Aulus Persius Flaccus," *Dial,* I, No. 1 (July, 1840), 117–21.

6. This was published in the *Dial,* Vol. IV, No. 3 (January, 1844).

7. Much of this material went into the essay, "The Service."

8. In the published journal, *Writings,* VII, 94; November 8, 1839, there are two brief quotations from the *Prometheus* given as examples of laconic speech. *Manuscript Journals* (*MA. 1302*) October 22, 1837–December 2, 1839, contain a brief of the whole play, alternating summary and translation. The passages given in English translation are lines 23–5, 88–92, 213–15, 446–68, 684–6, 717–27, and 1091–3 (the last three lines). These include Kratos' weak attempt to comfort Prometheus as he binds him to the rock; Prometheus' despairing cry, "Behold me,—what, a God, I suffer at the hands of Gods"; Prometheus' account to the chorus of his misfortunes, his wisdom, and his philanthropy toward mankind; Io's request to know what the future holds for her, and Prometheus' revelation (largely geographical and apparently interesting to Thoreau in the same way as the journey of the messengers to Achilles' tent in the *Iliad;* he calls it a passage of

next year he had gone on to the *Seven against Thebes*.[9] He commented as usual upon the simplicity of the poet's life[1] and language;[2] the wild Aeschylean scenery seemed to make an impression on him;[3] he admired the fresh and childlike wonder of the men of early days; he had little to say of the content of either play.[4] But both are heroic plays, and Thoreau must have found in *Prometheus,* at least, many qualities for his brave man; intelligence, benevolence toward mankind, courage in suffering, and indomitable determination.[5]

Thoreau had read Horace in college, his *Odes, Satires,* and *Epistles.* Now, writing on bravery, he equated bravery and virtue and recalled the quotation from Horace, *mea virtute me involvo*.[6] He went rapidly through the four books of the *Odes* to see what else he might find for his purpose. He found nothing to transfer bodily to the journal, but he copied into his commonplace book three pages of selections from Horace, mostly from Horace's *carpe diem* lines![7] It seems a puzzling selection, and when we remember that Thoreau once gave Horace as an example of a poet who led a solitary life, we are tempted to wonder whether he might possibly have misunderstood Horace. But the clue comes in two notes of Thoreau's which show very plainly that he was simply reading his own meaning into Horace's words. After the quota-

---

"lively narration"!) ; and Prometheus' last prayer to his mother, Ether, as the world begins to rock. This is apparently the beginning of Thoreau's translation of the entire play published in the *Dial,* Vol. III, No. 3 (January, 1843), and in *Writings,* v, 337–75. I have not been able to identify the text which he used for Aeschylus. See Supplement to App. A, No. 11.

9. *Writings,* VII, 116; journal of January 29, 1840. Sanborn says (*The Life of Henry David Thoreau,* p. 245, n. 1) that Thoreau read this play in college. I can find no evidence to support this statement.

1. *Writings,* VII, 93; journal of November 5, 1839: "There was one man who lived his own healthy Attic life in those days . . . like every genius, he was a solitary liver and worker in his day." *Ibid.,* VII, 117; journal of January 29, 1840: "The social condition of genius is the same in all ages. Aeschylus was undoubtedly alone and without sympathy in his simple reverence for the mystery of the universe."

2. *Ibid.,* VII, 94; journal of November 8, 1839: "Such naked speech is the standing aside of words to make room for thoughts." See also *ibid.,* VII, 116–17.

3. *Ibid.,* III, 70; "Ktaadn."

4. *Ibid.,* VII, 116–17; journal of January 29, 1840. The translation of *Prometheus Bound* in the *Dial* is prefaced by editorial comment which calls the play "a great old allegory," "a mystical picture of human life," and following Coleridge, "tragedy itself, in the plenitude of the idea." Whether Thoreau was in any way responsible for this comment is not known.

5. Thoreau later referred to Promethean energy (*Writings,* v, 156) and drew passing parallels between Prometheus and Christ (*ibid.,* I, 67; VIII, 390).

6. *Ibid.,* VII, 106; "Bravery and Music." See App. B, "Horace," for identification of quotation.

7. *College Note-Book* (MA. *594*), pp. 55ʳ–56ʳ. They can be generally dated by their appearance before an entry of February 10, 1840. See also *Writings,* VI, 27–31; letter to Helen, January 23, 1840, quoting with variation portions of nature description from *Odes* i, 4, 9. For all quotations from Horace, see App. B, "Horace." For discussion of text see Supplement to App. A, No. 8. In the quotations given here, I have followed Thoreau's transcript rather than standard text.

tion, *Culpam Poena premit comes,* Thoreau wrote, "Truer than was meant," and after the last quotation,

> Paulum sepultae distat inertiae
> Celata virtus,

he added his own comment, *alio sensu.* While Horace was simply urging Lollius to permit himself to be eulogized, Thoreau's interpretation of the lines, that the brave, the virtuous man must take his public stand, is written at length in the journal comments on bravery and in "The Service."

And *alio sensu* is the way in which Thoreau read all of Horace. Horace's *carpe diem* meant "Life is short; let us be happy"; Thoreau's meant "Life is short; let us not waste it." When we look at the selections again, in Thoreau's sense, their connection with bravery and wisdom is very clear. There is discussion of *vera virtus; vis* is refined into *vim temperatam;* the upright man enjoys his *probam pauperiam.* There is the man *justum et tenacem propositi* and the other one

> Ille potens sui
> Laetusque deget—, cui licet in diem
> Dixisse "Vixi":

men whom no reversals of fortune or thunderbolts of Jove could cause to tremble or to swerve. The poet himself, *Integer vitae scelerisque purus,* whose virtue and song saved him from harm, is missing from the pages, but he must have been in Thoreau's thoughts for he goes always with the other two; and if Thoreau found the tale too frivolous, still he adopted the connection between bravery and music, made music the accompaniment of every brave deed and the brave man music's sole patron.

From Horace it was an easy step to Persius.[8] In the introduction to his satires Persius proclaimed that he had never felt the poetic inspiration and was only half a poet, and Thoreau agreed with him. He denied to satire the distinction of poetry and to Persius the divinity of the poet. But he found some few ideas worth attention: from the first satire, that fame is not the chief end for which noble deeds should be done; from the second, that conformity to custom is not necessarily a sign of true virtue. He seemed especially interested in the third satire, in which the poet points out the folly of the young man who wastes his youth in vice and neglects the acquisition of learning. In the fifth satire Thoreau found those lines which speak of philosophy as teaching wisdom and a way of life.[9]

8. There are extracts from Persius accompanied by comment in the *College Note-Book,* pp. 61r–61v. An essay on Persius containing a few extracts appears in *Writings,* I, 327–33. The same essay was published in the *Dial,* Vol. I, No. I (July, 1840). For quotation from Persius see App. B, "Persius."

9. Thoreau found two lines only (Persius, *Satires* 3, 5–6) which he said might entitle the author to the epithet "Poet of Nature."

In general, however, he found Persius too bitter, too harsh, too violent. He was a buzzing, stinging, malicious sort of fellow; there was about him nothing of the calmness and serenity of the truly wise and great. Still, he might furnish Thoreau with material for an article; he might, by a kind of negative process, teach innocence, bravery, and virtue; and Thoreau could, when he chose, misread him as he had misread Horace. He took the lines,

> Est aliquid quo tendis, et in quod dirigis arcum?
> An passim sequeris corvos, testave, lutove,
> Securus quo pes ferat, atque ex tempore vivis?[1]

and admitting that Persius intended them as a reproach to the sluggard, made them instead the "motto of a wise man," secure in his innocence.

One sentence from Thoreau's criticism of Persius is worth repetition: "But the divinest poem, or the life of a great man, is the severest satire . . ."[2] This definition of a poem was an idea that was to grow upon Thoreau. He was to follow this statement with others much like it: "He is the true artist whose life is his material . . ."[3] "The true poem is not that which the public read. There is always a poem not printed on paper, coincident with the production of this, which is stereotyped in the poet's life, is what he has become through his work."[4] Before this, Thoreau had studied a poet's life as a check on his credentials to see whether he might be worth reading or as a final test of his sincerity to see whether he had believed his words enough to live them. But here is the suggestion that living is more important than writing, that action takes precedence over words, that a man does not write his poem in any but a secondary sense, that primarily he acts it.

Each author had contributed something to the portrait of the brave man: Aeschylus, wisdom, courage, determination; Horace, virtue and song; Persius, negatively and indirectly, innocence, confidence, and action. Others made minor contributions. Vergil offered from antiquity the modern transcendental doctrine of beauty of scene added to beauty of deed. The good, according to Thoreau and Vergil, dwelt "in a more precious light than other men."

> Largior hic campos aether et lumine vestit
> Purpureo: Solemque suum, sua sidera norunt.[5]

1. *Writings*, I, 331; Persius, *Satires* 3, 61–3.
2. *Writings*, I, 329.
3. *Ibid.*, VII, 149; journal of January 23, 1840.
4. *Ibid.*, VII, 157; journal of July 1, 1840. See also *ibid.*, VII, 153, 167.
5. *Ibid.*, VII, 120; journal of February 15, 1840. See also *ibid.*, VI, 28; letter to Helen, January 23, 1840: *Majoresque cadunt de montibus umbrae.* The first quotation is from the *Aeneid,* the second from the *Eclogues.* See App. B, "Vergil," for location. It would be difficult to make any deductions about Thoreau's reading in Vergil at this time from these two quotations.

Xenophon furnished the wise sayings of the Seven Sages of Athens.[6] Even Cudworth, whose English history of philosophy Thoreau was reading with a mixture of tolerance and skepticism,[7] offered a few philosophic deeds and words, and the journal was liberally sprinkled with anecdotes and aphorisms drawn from a wide variety of sources and illustrative of the conduct and conversation of the brave.[8]

Plutarch naturally made the greatest single contribution, for the *Lives* abound in "brave traits" and the *Moralia* in wise sayings.[9] And he not only contributed specific incident and comment but furnished Thoreau with two tools for his investigation of reality: a theory of history and a theory of philosophy. When Thoreau was reading Homer he had been pleased to accept myth as truth; now, reading the *Lives* which chronicle events only as men have reacted to them, he inclined to believe that the events themselves were unimportant and that only the courage and wisdom—or the lack of them—with which men met events had value as history, that history became truth only as it approached the mythical or apocryphal:

The value of many traits in Grecian history depends not so much on their importance in history, as [on] the readiness with which they accept a wide interpretation, and illustrate the poetry and ethics of mankind. When they announce no particular truth, they are yet central to all truth. They are like those examples by which we improve, but of which we never formally extract the moral.[1]

Thoreau was beginning to be aware of the very indefinite quality of knowledge. As the communication had failed to come in words, he had transposed it to music and etherealized it into silence. As he had failed to find the full measure of truth in poetry, he had believed it to lie in

6. *Writings*, vii, 141; journal of June 16, 1840. The seven sages engage in an extended discussion of love and friendship at their banquet.

7. *Ibid.*, vii, 133; journal of April 9, 1840; *ibid.*, vii, 150.

8. The references to Thales (*Writings*, vii, 134, 163) and the list of aphoristic quotations (*ibid.*, vii, 139) were probably from some philosophical reading in English. References to Pittacus and Bias (consult App. C for location) might have come from a number of sources, classical or otherwise.

9. The stories of Solon and Cylon (*Writings*, vii, 164, 165) come from Plutarch, *Life of Solon* x, xii. Anecdotes from the *Moralia* appear in *Writings*, vii, 100, 105–6 (*Moralia* ii, 254); this is incorrectly identified by the editors of the journals as "Roman Questions" lxviii; it is *ibid.*, lxxviii; and *Moralia* i, 171–2, "On Superstition." There are also scattered selections from the *Moralia* in the *College Note-Book* (*MA. 594*), pp. 76r–76v. I give them with titles, cue words, and location in the edition of the *Moralia* listed in App. A, No. 36: "A Discourse Concerning Socrates's Daemon": ". . . every Soul hath some Portion of Reason . . . call it a Daemon . . ." (*Moralia* ii, 409); "Of Man's Progress in Vertue": "This Antiphanes said merrily . . . vigorous Summer of their Age." (*Moralia* ii, 454); "Of Man's Progress in Vertue"; " 'Twas handsomely said of *Diogenes* . . . in the Tavern . . ." (*Moralia* ii, 463–4); "That a Philosopher ought Chiefly to Converse with great Men": "But these Men have taken . . . and inflexible resolution." (*Moralia* ii, 371.)

1. *Writings*, vii, 165; journal of July 9, 1840.

the poet's life. When the facts of history had seemed to him trivial, he had found mythology significant. Reading philosophy, he had found no answer to his questions. Plato and Aristotle and Cudworth had given him dogma, not a way of life. But Plutarch gave him a theory he could use, a definition of philosophy which he could endorse:

. . . the true philosophy . . . is a Spring and Principle of *Motion* whenever it comes; it makes Men active and industrious, it sets every *Wheel* and faculty a going, it stores our *Minds* with Axioms and Rules, by which to make a sound Judgment, it determines the *Will* to the Choice of what is honorable and just.[2]

Thoreau was about to change his method of procedure, but he would not abandon his former ideas. He reaffirmed his own centrality;[3] he restated his concept of the poet;[4] characteristically he exhorted himself to patience, insisting that his dissatisfaction was but a sign of high expectation.[5] Still the dissatisfaction persisted. He seemed willing, almost eager, to adapt himself to, to make trial of, the ways of the world. Everything pointed to action: the slowness of revelation, the satisfactions of his activity in the world and his associations with people, the outward direction of writing for publication rather than for eternity, the reading he was doing in the classical authors. In midsummer of 1840 he wrote in his journal, "Let us not wait any longer, but step down from the mountains on to the plain of the earth. . . . It concerns us rather to be something here present than to leave something behind us."[6] Within a few days he abandoned the journal; in the fall he copied a very significant quotation into his commonplace book, a quotation from an article in a current periodical: "Facts may be *true,* and views may be *true,* but they are not *Truth.* Truth is *Sincere Being* . . ."[7]

A few months later Thoreau had moved from the world of theory to the world of activity. In the first entry of 1841 he reported his satisfaction.

A day is lapsing. . . . I hear busy feet on the floors, and the whole house jars with industry. . . . The momentous topics of human life are always of secondary importance to the business in hand . . . The squeaking of the pump sounds as necessary as the music of the spheres. . . . The solidity and apparent necessity of this routine insensibly recommend it to me. . . . Routine is a ground to stand on, a wall to retreat to . . .[8]

2. *College Note-Book* (*MA. 594*), p. 76ʳ; *Moralia* ii, 371.
3. *Writings*, vii, 84; journal of July 11, 1839.
4. *Ibid.*, vii, 74–5.
5. *Ibid.*, vii, 92, 146.
6. *Ibid.*, vii, 167; journal of July 11, 1840.
7. *Literary Note-Book*, p. 22.
8. *Writings*, vii, 173; journal of January 23, 1841. At Walden Thoreau was to change his mind on this subject, using almost the same words to convey an opposite conviction. See *ibid.*, i, 229–30.

He was only twenty-four; he could not hold himself forever to an ascetic discipline.

By spells seriousness will be forced to cut capers, and drink a deep and refreshing draft of silliness . . . Like overtasked schoolboys, all my members and nerves and sinews petition Thought for a recess, and my very thighbones itch to slip away from under me, and run and join the *mêlée*. I exult in stark inanity, leering on nature and the soul.[9]

He was impatient of books, critical even of Homer and Aeschylus and Dante.[1] A good book taught him better than to read it. He must put it down and live on its hint.[2] After an illness in February he experienced that sharpened sense of aliveness that comes with recovery. All sounds delighted him: the lowing of cattle, the threshing in the barn, the tinkling of the anvil, cowbells and horns, the barking of dogs. His sense of sight seemed sharpened too. "How much virtue there is in simply seeing!"[3] Pictures stood out sharp and clear: the snow on the trees, the trail of a fox, horse and oxen standing by woodpiles in the forest. There was sheer jubilance in his words: "My life at this moment is like a summer morning when birds are singing."[4] "Life looks as fair at this moment as a summer's sea, or a blond dress in a saffron light . . ."[5]

The journal held fewer comments on the mystery and more on duty and conduct; there was criticism of Lyceum programs, the lecturers and the audience; there was more nature and less Nature; the mystic communion became drowsing in the sun.

The eaves are running on the south side of the house; the titmouse lisps in the poplar; the bells are ringing for church; while the sun presides over all and makes his simple warmth more obvious than all else. What shall I do with this hour, so like time and yet so fit for eternity? . . . I lie out indistinct as a heath at noonday. I am evaporating and ascending into the sun.[6]

When in March he wrote his interpretation of Emerson's poem, "The Sphinx," he wrote his own interpretation of man's eternal quest and his own conclusion that there would not be an answer in words, but only in the soul of man. With this he seemed not dissatisfied.

He became so very practical that he thought of buying a farm; in March and April he argued the matter with himself and was finally saved from the step by external circumstance. Late in April he went instead to live at Emerson's.

9. *Ibid.*, VII, 175; journal of January 24, 1841.
1. *Ibid.*, VII, 218; journal of February 20, 1841.
2. *Ibid.*, VII, 216; journal of February 19, 1841.
3. *Ibid.*, VII, 247; journal of April 10, 1841.
4. *Ibid.*, VII, 210; journal of February 9, 1841.
5. *Ibid.*, VII, 224; journal of February 27, 1841. Saffron is a strange color, but it was a favorite color with the Romans. Notice also the feminine quality of the simile.
6. *Ibid.*, VII, 203–4; journal of February 7, 1841. See also *ibid.*, v, 173.

There he came back into the world of thought, not his own original thought but the standard popular thought of the literary and intellectual circle. It is amusing to see him borrowing Emerson's commonplace book and transferring sections of it to his own.[7] What he borrowed from Emerson probably meant little to him, for little of it ever escaped from the covers of the notebook. This was true also of the reading which he did under Emersonian influence and probably from the Emersonian library.[8] The Thomas Taylor translations of the classics were favorites of the transcendentalists, and the kind of thing which made transcendentalist reading was favorite material for Taylor. Taylor translated an imposing array of classical works, but he was especially interested in the mystic writings and in Platonic and Neoplatonic philosophy. It was inevitable that he would translate and that transcendentalists would read Jamblichus' *Life of Pythagoras,* for Pythagoras held the belief that the soul was divine and taught the investigation of nature as a way of life that led to truth. Porphyry derived his importance from his discipleship to Plotinus, and his *On Abstinence from Animal Food* was very widely read and sometimes followed by those who would discipline the body to strengthen the soul.

Thoreau, however, was not interested in any metaphysical solution of the universe, and the *Life of Pythagoras* left hardly a trace in the journal. Most of the selections in Thoreau's notebook were philosophically nontechnical and dealt with Pythagoras' advice to his followers on problems of conduct.[9] One, however, Thoreau must have liked because it furnished him proof of the reality of his mystic experiences and of their relation to sphere music.

Pythagoras, however, did not procure for himself a thing of the kind through instruments or the voice, but employing a certain ineffable divinity, and which it is difficult to apprehend, he extended his ears, and fixed his intellect in the sublime symphonies of the world, he alone hearing and understanding, as it appears, the universal harmony and consonance of the spheres, and the stars that are moved through them, and which produce a fuller and more intense melody than any thing effected by mortal sounds.[1]

7. *Literary Note-Book,* pp. 53 ff.
8. On April 18, 1841, Thoreau recorded in *HM13201,* p. 21, his intention of reading five books, among them Jamblichus' *Life of Pythagoras,* Porphyry's *On Abstinence from Animal Food,* and Bode's *Orpheus.* The reading was realized in the *Literary Note-Book,* pp. 11–51. For description of these books see App. A, Nos. 39, 41–2.
9. The selections from Jamblichus come from Taylor (see App. A, No. 41), pp. 9–12, on the journey of Pythagoras to Egypt; p. 35, on advice to women on not domineering over their husbands; p. 44, on Pythagoras' hearing the divine symphonies of the universe; p. 183, on living and dying well; p. 198, on prosperity attending intellect (also in *Writings,* I, 338). There are also a number of Pythagorean sayings from varied sources which appear in Taylor, pp. 259–60, 261, 264, 267, 270, 271, 272. The *Literary Note-Book,* pp. 41–3, contains several Pythagorean fragments which I have been unable to find in Taylor or in other usual sources.
1. *Literary Note-Book,* p. 31; Taylor, p. 44.

Of the Porphyry there was no immediate sign in the journal; there is, however, some evidence in *Walden* that Porphyry did not leave Thoreau totally unimpressed.[2]

Along with the Jamblichus and the Porphyry, Thoreau read both about and from Orpheus. Orpheus appealed to the transcendentalists because of his mysticism; he answered Thoreau's own desire to go back beyond the historical to the traditional and mythical. Thoreau apparently read Orpheus in the original and translated favorite passages for his notebook. There are a great many of these selections on varying subjects and unaccompanied by comment,[3] but Orpheus appears in the journals only in casual references as the mythological inventor of music and in Thoreau's other writings indirectly as the inspiration for the Orphics and for the apostrophe to Diana.

Thoreau was not a follower either in reading or living, and the life of social and literary conformity palled. By May he was writing in the journal, "Life in gardens and parlors is unpalatable to me,"[4] and in July to Lucy Brown, "I grow savager and savager every day, as if fed on raw meat, and my tameness is only the repose of untamableness."[5] By fall he found poetry "tame and partial"; he was disgusted with himself that he looked for it in libraries rather than in the fields; only Homer satisfied him at all, served him for escape: "We read him with a rare sense of freedom and irresponsibleness, as though we trod on native ground, and were autochthones of the soil."[6] His yearning for the wild increased. In December he was making his plans: "I want to go soon and live away by the pond . . . I don't want to feel as if my life were a sojourn any longer. . . . It is time now that I begin to live."[7]

But before he could carry out his plans, on January 11, 1842, his brother John died, and the soul of the young philosopher was sadly shaken. Three years out of college, he had tried self-communion, he had tried literature, he had tried the active life; he had come without too much pain to feel that there might be no revelation that could be set

2. There is perhaps an allusion to Porphyry in the comment of the next year on the grossness of the kitchen (*Writings,* VII, 311; January 3, 1842). See also *ibid.,* II, 232–46; *Walden,* "Higher Laws"; and *ibid.,* I, 237.

3. He read a part of Bode's *Orpheus* (for description see App. A, No. 39) and copied from an unidentified text into the *Literary Note-Book,* pp. 44–51, these selections: *Argonautica,* 232–75 (launching of the Argo), 365–73 (beginning of the voyage); *Hymns,* 4 (of the Ether), 6 (of the Stars), 7 (of the Sun), 19 (of Zeus, the thunderer), 33 (of Victory), 40 (of Ceres), 42 (of the Seasons), 68 (of Hygeia), 77 (of Dawn), 81 (of Zephyr), 83 (of the Ocean), 85 (of Sleep), 86 (of Dream), and the fragment on the unity and completeness of Zeus, attributed to Philemon. Thoreau has not given entire hymns in most cases but only a few lines.

4. *Writings,* VII, 256; journal of May 1, 1841.

5. *Ibid.,* VI, 36; letter of July 21, 1841. Lucy Brown was a sister to Lidian Emerson and had visited in Concord.

6. *Ibid.,* VII, 284; journal of September 5, 1841.

7. *Ibid.,* VII, 299; journal of December 24, 25, 1841.

down in words but that there might be a steady revelation of feeling, of spirit, of consciousness, of communion with the universe, a revelation of conviction rather than of reason. He was devising another plan, to go and live by the pond, where he could once more try to study himself and nature. But John died and all his beliefs and purposes seemed empty. From January 9 until February 19 there was no writing in the journal. When Thoreau sat down to write again he wrote in a few words the record of the last years:

My path hitherto has been like a road through a diversified country, now climbing high mountains, then descending into the lowest vales. From the summits I saw the heavens; from the vales I looked up to the heights again. In prosperity I remember God . . . in adversity I remember my own elevations, and only hope to see God again.[8]

It was difficult for a transcendentalist to admit the depth of his grief; in transcendental theory our "friends" are sent to teach us certain things, and when we have learned our lessons our friends are withdrawn. Writing to Lucy Brown, Thoreau tried hard to maintain that point of view and to feel the wonder of such an ordering of things.[9] Even in the journal he tried to maintain the pretense, or perhaps rather to convince himself. There was no word of John in the journal. There were few words of death: impersonal observations on the death of a "friend"; sometimes, turning the knife in the wound, comparison of the death of "the animal" to that of the vegetable; restatement of the idea that we are given experience that we may learn; once, a sudden sharp realization of death as personal extinction;[1] but half hidden among great blocks of literary criticism and plaints on waning friendships there ran the record of a serious struggle, of alternate rebellion and resignation, calm and despair. Like other mortals, Thoreau beat against the closed gates and voiced the old, old question: Why? This time he needed the answer. And, as always, there was silence.

I was always conscious of sounds in nature which my ears could never hear,— that I caught but the prelude to a strain. She always retreats as I advance. Away behind and behind is she and her meaning. Will not this faith and expectation make to itself ears at length? I never saw to the end, nor heard to the end; but the best part was unseen and unheard.[2]

There is no sadder entry than that of March 11; his resignation is hard won and short lived.

8. *Ibid.*, vii, 320; journal of February 20, 1842.
9. *Ibid.*, vi, 41–3; letter of March 2, 1842.
1. *Ibid.*, vii, 339; journal of March 19, 1842: "I see laws which **never** fail, of whose failure I never conceived. Indeed I cannot detect failure anywhere but in my fear. I do not fear that right is not right, that good is not good, but only the annihilation of the present existence. But only that can make me incapable of fear."
2. *Ibid.*, vii, 321; journal of February 21, 1842.

I must receive my life as passively as the willow leaf that flutters over the brook. . . . I feel as if [I] could at any time resign my life and the responsibility of living into God's hands, and become as innocent, free from care, as a plant or stone.

My life! My life! why will you linger? Are the years short and the months of no account? How often has long delay quenched my aspirations! . . . Why were my ears given to hear those everlasting strains which haunt my life, and yet to be prophaned much more by these perpetual dull sounds?

Our doubts are so musical that they persuade themselves.

Why, God, did you include me in your great scheme? Will you not make me a partner at last?[3]

On March 26 he could write in the old vein of conviction, "I am time and the world. . . . In me are summer and winter, village life and commercial routine, pestilence and famine and refreshing breezes, joy and sadness, life and death," and two paragraphs later, "Where is my heart gone? They say men cannot part with it and live."[4]

John was dead and Henry's heart was gone. Bewildered, Henry could only wonder at the alternate pain and pleasure of life, a life "too strange for sorrow . . . too strange for joy."[5] But even in his grief he would not abandon the conviction of God's essential goodness: "I thank God for sorrow. It is hard to be abused. Is not He kind still, who lets this south wind blow, this warm sun shine on me?"[6]

Whether Thoreau could no longer write in his journal or whether he destroyed it, there is no journal from April 3, 1842, to July 5, 1845, among the manuscript journals which he preserved.[7] But writing for

3. *Ibid.*, VII, 326–7; journal of March 11, 1842. See also *ibid.*, VII, 338–9.
4. *Ibid.*, VII, 349–50; journal of March 26, 1842.
5. *Ibid.*, VII, 351–2; journal of March 27, 1842.
6. *Ibid.*, VII, 358; journal of April 3, 1842.
7. The Manuscript Journals (*MA. 1302*) in the Morgan Library contain slightly more material than the fourteen published volumes, but they are not complete. Parts of pages and whole sheaves of pages have been torn from the books, and there are great gaps in the 1840's. It may be significant that there is so little record for the 1842–45 period and again for the years 1848–50, for these seem to have been periods of great disturbance in Thoreau's life, so that it would be reasonable to conjecture that he either did not keep his journal with his usual thoroughness or that he later destroyed much of it. It would also be a reasonable theory that he so ravished the pre- and post-Walden journals for material for *The Week* and *Walden* that it seemed foolish to preserve the scraps. There are, however, *Huntington Journal Fragments* (*HM13182*) which come from precisely these two periods, which contain material of a rather personal nature, material emotional enough so that it is badly written and might therefore have been discarded for more than one reason. According to Sanborn (*The First and Last Journeys of Thoreau*, I, 121) these were fragments which Sophia held separate from the rest of the journals in her disposition of her brother's manuscript and left with relatives named Thatcher, the assumption being that she did not wish them to become public property. Sanborn has printed large sections of them in his *The First and Last Journeys of Thoreau*, but he has rearranged them and has omitted most material that seems personal in character.

the public was an outward matter, a kind of protection from himself, and a way of keeping busy. It is in the publications of the next few years that we must follow him. These were of two types: lectures and essays made up of extracts from the earlier journals, and articles written from current reading expressly for publication; in other words, they were not the "natural fruit" of reading, observation, and thought.

July, 1842, saw the publication in the *Dial* of an article called "The Natural History of Massachusetts," a review of a state bulletin, decorated with nature notes from the journal and with two translations of Anacreon which Thoreau had done in 1839. The October *Dial* published eight of Thoreau's own poems. In January, 1843, he contributed to the magazine extracts from the *Laws of Menu*, which he had previously read, and the translation of *Prometheus Bound*, begun so long ago. This month he wrote to Lucy Brown, referring indirectly to his grief and depression but insisting that he was happier than he could reasonably expect to be.[8] He lectured at the Lyceum on Sir Walter Raleigh, using at last the great mass of notes that he had been accumulating for several years. And he began to read the Greek minor poets, securing the book from the Fruitlands collection.[9] This reading was evident almost immediately in a large group of translations from Anacreon in the *Dial* for April.[1] The April issue of the *Dial* is said to have been edited almost entirely by Thoreau. He certainly contributed liberally to it: the Anacreon translations, selections from the *Ethnical Scriptures*, several poems, including the Orphics "Smoke" and "Haze," and an essay, "The Dark Ages," taken substantially from reading and notes of 1837–38.

Early in May Thoreau left Emerson's house to go as a tutor into the household of William Emerson in New York.[2] He was ill shortly after his arrival and had difficulty driving himself to work. He was homesick, although he stoutly denied it. He went on reading English poetry, working on the translation of the *Seven against Thebes*, which he finished but did not publish, and going from Anacreon to Pindar among the Greek lyrists.[3]

In the fall the *Dial* printed another installment of *Ethnical Scriptures* and the essay "A Winter Walk," another rearrangement of journal material.[4] The *Boston Miscellany* accepted "The Walk to Wachusett,"

8. *Writings*, VI, 46–8, letter of January 25, 1843.
9. *Writings*, VI, 60; letter to Emerson, February 15, 1843. See App. A, No. 40.
1. The *Dial*, III, No. 4 (April, 1843), 484–90. This is approximately the same essay which appears in *Writings*, I, 238–44.
2. See Thoreau's letters (*Writings*, VI, 68–119) for details of his life in New York. There is also a journal of about fifty pages which belongs to this period in the *Huntington Journal Fragments*, parts of which Sanborn has published in *The First and Last Journeys of Thoreau*.
3. *Writings*, VI, 102; letter to Emerson, August 7, 1843. See App. A, No. 37.
4. This contained the translation of the snowflake simile from the *Iliad*.

an account of an event of 1842; and the *Democratic Review* took an essay, "The Landlord," and the review of Etzler's book, *Paradise to be Regained*. These last two articles belong to the group of those written rather than simply arranged and revised for publication, and both of them show traces of Thoreau's current thinking. "The Landlord" is a rather weakly romantic essay, idealizing its subject into a kind of Golden Age farmer and reflecting Thoreau's loneliness for the country. The review of Etzler's book indicates Thoreau's returning spiritual strength; in it he objects to the importance attached to the material and mechanical aspects of civilization and is willing to do verbal battle for his convictions. It is his first outward sign of social conscience.

Thoreau's friends had urged him to go to New York; they thought it would make him less narrow and provincial. But Concord meant more to him than any other place; in New York he might write, he might meet the men of the day, he might establish contacts with publishers, he might frequent libraries; but he was unhappy, he did not find the Emersons sympathetic, he hated cities, he was ill physically and depressed mentally, he wanted to be at home. By fall he was back in his father's house, helping with the family business, writing a little on the side. In November he gave the lecture on poetry that had been in preparation almost since his first journal comments on Homer, and in January, 1844, it was published in the *Dial* under the title "Homer. Ossian. Chaucer." The same issue contained a group of Thoreau's translations of Pindar. Thoreau had not too high an opinion of Pindar;[5] the translations appeared without any comment by him but with editorial comment explaining that they were taken from Mr. Thoreau's notebooks at the request of readers who had admired his Aeschylus and Anacreon translations and regretting that Pindar, despite his high poetical reputation, did not adapt well to English. The selections were generally characteristic of Thoreau's interests: some were mythological; most were, naturally, glorifications of heroes with occasional scenic accompaniments of natural beauty—again the beauty of the scene enhancing the beauty of the deed. Thoreau was pleased to discover that Pindar entertained the same lofty regard for poetry as was held by Sidney, by the transcendentalists, and by Henry D. Thoreau.[6]

In the April *Dial* Thoreau's social conscience again asserted itself. He wrote a commendatory notice of an abolitionist paper called the *Herald of Freedom*.[7] He made other unimportant contributions to this issue: a few more fragments from Pindar, two collections of oriental

5. *Writings*, VI, 102.
6. *Ibid.*, IV, 392.
7. Another later indication of awakening social conscience occurs in Thoreau's account of Wendell Phillips before the Concord Lyceum, March 12, 1845, in a letter to the editor of the *Liberator* (*Writings*, IV, 311-15).

scripture. As Thoreau had written Emerson the year before, the *Ethnical Scriptures* were holding out surprisingly well.[8]

In addition to the heavy classical translation of these years, there is classical quotation or reference in nearly every article. Most of the quotations are familiar ones, repeated only; in "The Walk to Wachusett," however, there is quotation from Vergil indicative of new reading.[9] In 1841 Homer had represented to Thoreau an escape from the tameness of his life; now after John's death the classics seem to have afforded him a certain solace. There was about them that remoteness, detachment, and serenity that he needed. He wrote in his comment on Anacreon, "I know of no studies so composing as those of the classical scholar. When we have sat down to them, life seems as still and serene as if it were very far off . . . Reading the classics . . . is like walking amid the stars and constellations, a high and by way serene to travel."[1]

That is Thoreau's record from 1842 to 1845, years filled with inner idleness and surface activity. As he began to recover, he must have wanted something better. Mrs. Marble has quoted a letter written in 1843 by a relative of Thoreau's referring to him in these words: "I think he is getting to view things more as others do than formerly,—he remarked he had been studying books, now he intended to study nature and daily life. It would be well!"[2] This time someone else was reading his meaning into Thoreau's words. The writer surmised that Thoreau would go to work; Thoreau went to Walden.

8. *Writings*, VI, 114; October 17, 1843.
9. *Ibid.*, V, 138, 144–5. See App. B, "Vergil."
1. *Ibid.*, I, 238–9.
2. Annie Russell Marble, *Thoreau, His Home, Friends and Books* (New York, T. Y. Crowell, 1902), p. 144.

III

The Homeric Experiment

"Both place and time were changed, and I dwelt nearer to those parts of the universe and to those eras in history which had most attracted me."

ON July 4, 1845, Thoreau took up his residence at Walden to stay until Stepember 6, 1847. For the record of these two years there are seventy-seven pages of journal, *The Week,* and *Walden.*[1] The journal is in two parts: a journal of forty-one pages dated from July 5, 1845 to March 27, 1846, and a small, badly mutilated journal which can be assigned to no more specific date than the Walden period.[2] In the journal, which has always the peculiar value of a private document, Thoreau himself recognized two limitations, its incompleteness[3] and its lack of connection and continuity. He made a very acute analysis of this second defect, acknowledging his inability to make the proper connection between his thoughts even after he had polished and perfected their expression.

From all points of the compass, from the earth beneath and the heavens above, have come these inspirations and been entered duly in the order of their arrival in the journal. Thereafter, when the time arrived, they were winnowed into lectures, and again, in due time, from lectures into essays. And at last they stand, like the cubes of Pythagoras, firmly on either basis; like statues on their pedestals, but the statues rarely take hold of hands. There is only such connection and series as is attainable in the galleries. And this affects their immediate and popular influence.[4]

Everyone who reads Thoreau feels this lack of connection, this clarity of the part but not of the whole. The incoherence of the journals, coupled

1. The essay "Carlyle and his Works," *Writings,* IV, 316–55, published in *Graham's Magazine* for March and April, 1847, also belongs to this period. Much of it appears elsewhere in Thoreau's writings; it contains a few general classical allusions of no significance for this study.

2. There is also a journal dated simply 1837–47; this is printed in *Writings,* VII, 436–88. There are a few scraps in the *Huntington Journal Fragments* (*HM13182*) which may possibly belong to the Walden years.

3. *Writings,* I, 354.

4. *Ibid.,* VII, 413; 1845–47. See also *ibid.,* VII, 199–200; IX, 239. The figure of the cubes of Pythagoras seems to come from Hierocles' comment on Socrates' speech (unidentified Pythagorean fragment, *Literary Note-Book,* p. 42) and from the Pythagorean fragment from Stobaeus (*ibid.,* p. 32; Taylor's *Jamblichus,* p. 260).

with their incompleteness—with Thoreau's deliberate practice of omitting the circumstance which occasioned the thought—makes it easy for the casual reader to miss the story in the journals. These defects are a serious impediment to any synthesis of Thoreau's thought, and they are present not only in the journal but even in *The Week* and *Walden,* which constitute his most serious attempts to organize and summarize.

The Week, prepared for publication at Walden and published two years later in 1849, is half travelogue and half a summary of Thoreau's opinions to date. Many times the expression of this opinion involves nothing more than the collection and arrangement of sentences and paragraphs from the earlier journals, but the inclusion of material in *The Week* puts the stamp of Thoreau's current approval upon it and marks it as the enduring part of the journal. In some cases we find the expressions in the journal modified in *The Week,* and then it becomes necessary to consider whether a change of thought is involved or whether the variation is simply the difference between public and private utterance. At any rate *The Week* reports Thoreau's eight— and more—years of thought and investigation, and despite its rambling style and loose organization it is detailed and specific in its information.

Walden, on the other hand, is much better organized and much more general; it does not promulgate any system of thought or of life. It is rather an invitation to men to live their own lives and to think their own thoughts. It is a practical handbook on basic living, written very simply for the inexperienced, offering facts and figures, and setting forth some of the obvious and immediate advantages of the life it advertises. It promises freedom from toil, restrictions, and worries; it paints the beauties of nature and the joys of the out-of-doors. Even the less immediately practical chapters are written on an elementary textbook level. In "Reading" Thoreau speaks of the value of books in general and of the relative values of different types of books. In "Sounds" he dwells on the sounds of the woods, the highway, and the village rather than on sphere music; he does not even mention here the cricket chant or the telegraph harp. In "Solitude" he emphasizes the joys of escaping from the annoyances of society more than the pleasures of attaining the solitude of the poet and the philosopher. *Walden,* like *The Week,* presents its technical problem. Although most of it, according to Thoreau's introductory statement in the book, was written at Walden, there is still a substantial amount of material which comes from the early 1850's and must not be assigned to 1845–47. These three documents, written in different techniques for different purposes, furnish the information for the Walden years.

Everyone will remember Thoreau's statements in *Walden* of his reasons for going to the woods. These were the published reasons: to live

fully, deeply, and deliberately; to *taste* life. On that level his years at
Walden were an experiment in reducing life to a proper material simplicity. But in the journal he said, "I wish to meet the facts of life—
the vital facts, which are the phenomena or actuality the gods meant
to show us—face to face, and so I came down here. Life! who knows
what it is, what it does?"[5] This was a personal confession. It was more
than the desire to prove life good or bad, more than the wish to live
simply and close to nature; it was the hope of finding the answer, of
discerning what lay behind the façade. For this was the private business
that Thoreau went to Walden to transact, that he could find no time for
in the trivia of everyday living. On this level his years at Walden were
another experiment in the search for truth. The success of the material
experiment was essential for the success of the spiritual one.

   This twofold freedom, from certain things and for others, Thoreau
had long yearned for. He knew what he wished to escape: the unnecessary and meaningless complications of contemporary civilization. He
knew what he hoped to find: an adequate explanation of life. Before
Walden he had managed to achieve this freedom on a vicarious and
temporary basis through reading the *Iliad*. His frequent references to
the enchantment it held for him, to its serenity, remoteness, and simplicity, indicate that it did serve him as a release from strain. What
Greece meant to him is fully and nostalgically, if not very poetically,
expressed in this poem.

> When life contracts into a vulgar span,
> And human nature tires to be a man,
>   I thank the gods for Greece,
>   That permanent realm of peace.
> For as the rising moon far in the night
> Checkers the shade with her forerunning light,
> So in my darkest hours my senses seem
>   To catch from her Acropolis a gleam.
>
>   Greece, who am I that should remember thee,
> Thy Marathon and thy Thermopylae?
> Is my life vulgar, my fate mean,
> Which on such golden memories can lean?[6]

   But the Greeks did more for Thoreau than the movies do for moderns. The cinema furnishes the negative freedom of anesthesia; Homer
furnished Thoreau with a positive pattern for free material and spiritual
living. His delight in the material simplicity of Homeric life has been
mentioned in connection with his earlier reading of the *Iliad*. The beautiful relaxation of reckoning time by the sun; of sitting down, tired from

5. *Writings*, VII, 362; journal of July 6, 1845.
6. *Ibid.*, V, 404.

work, to simple meals; of watching gods and goddesses glide effort-
lessly down mountains, of listening to the roar of the wine-dark sea has
an inevitable appeal for the man who must live his life by the clock, eat
his meals on a household schedule, travel via railway, and spend his days
making pencils. Thoreau's whole Walden experiment might very reasonably be interpreted as a conscious effort to realize the simplicity of
Homeric life.

It might also, of course, be interpreted as an attempt to realize the
life of oriental contemplation or the primitive life of the North American Indian. However, the Greek pattern of life offered Thoreau the
action which the oriental did not and the intellectuality which the Indian did not. He was interested in the primitive Indian but he regarded
the contemporary Indian with a very clear eye, and he was so far removed from any real sympathy with Indian life as to find hunting—
and even at times fishing—distasteful. He might be "at rare intervals"
a Yogi; but he really liked to think of himself as "a good Greek," and
he cultivated in himself the twin disciplines of mind and body for which
the Greeks were distinguished.

Thoreau's journal in the early days of the experiment indicates that
Greece and the classics were steadily in his thoughts. He thinks that his
house has the auroral atmosphere of the halls of Olympus, such an atmosphere as that in which the works of Grecian art were made;[7] natural
objects remind him of patterns in Greek art;[8] Walden is his Ithaca; he
is a fellow wanderer and survivor of Ulysses;[9] he is visited by a woodchopper, a true Homeric boor, a Paphlagonian man;[1] then come five
Lestrigones;[2] there are many passages of appreciation of the classics,
later transferred to *Walden*.[3]

It is here, I think, that we have the clue to the major classical influence operative in Thoreau's life. He found, certainly, many values
in his study of the classics: proofs of certain favorite theories, fragments
of truth in myth, patterns and styles for composition, and a strong
philological interest. But these were individual and more or less isolated benefits, while the Homeric philosophy spread out into his whole
life.

The Homeric philosophy involved not only a simplification of living
but also a simplification of thinking. Thoreau spoke with admiration
of the "free, and wild thinking" in the *Iliad*.[4] There was no cant in
Homer, he said, because there was no religion; men clung to his song

7. *Ibid.*, VII, 361; journal of July 5, 1845.
8. *Ibid.*, VII, 363; journal of July 7, 1845.
9. *Ibid.*
1. *Ibid.*, VII, 365; journal of July 14, 1845.
2. *Ibid.*, VII, 366; journal of July 14, 1845.
3. *Ibid.*, VII, 370, 371, 377; II, 111–14.
4. *Ibid.*, VIII, 97.

because they still had "moments of unbaptized and uncommitted life,
which give them an appetite for more." He repeated in *The Week* the
comment from the journal of 1841 : "The Iliad represents no creed nor
opinion, and we read it with a rare sense of freedom and irresponsibil-
ity . . ."[5] Just as a return to the primitive life appeals to human beings
beset with the machinery of civilization, so the living of a natural life
appeals to those who have struggled too long either with religious dogma
or with spiritual aspiration. When Thoreau compared the Grecian and
Hebrew theologies it was to the disadvantage of the Hebrew from both
of these points of view : he found the doctrine too rigid and Christ too
other-worldly.[6] He pitied the "poor inconsistent aspirant man, seeking
to live a pure life, feeding on air, divided against himself . . ."[7]

Thoreau was to some extent one of these poor aspirant men : otherwise he could not have realized their tragedy. It was a general tragedy
of the time. Thinking men had cut themselves loose from authority,
a courageous gesture but a pathetic one. They believed it was the duty
of every man to think for himself : they failed to realize the pitiful inadequacy of the human intellect. Cast adrift to depend upon themselves,
to hold to a stricter standard than their abandoned faith, to try one
rational theory after another to reconcile the contradictions in the universe and solve the eternal problem of the apparent evil in the world,
many scholars found an answer and release in the gently fatalistic
theology of the *Iliad*.[8] Homer relaxed the terrible necessity. He gave no
license to evil, but he offered tolerance and sympathy for humanity : he
removed the ugliness of judgment and the sorrow of guilt and remorse.
On the basis of fact, Helen was a loose woman : in spirit, she moved
through the pages of the *Iliad* a lovely and a gracious lady. So with all
of Homer's heroes and heroines : they moved with human weakness but
with dignity and courage, with gentle tolerance and sympathy for
each other, through a beautiful and incomprehensible world. They had

5. *Ibid.*, VII, 284 ; I, 394.
6. *Ibid.*, VII, 390–1 ; I, 65 ff., 74.
7. *Ibid.*, I, 35. For other statements on the healthiness of amorality and cowardice of
repentance see *ibid.*, II, 11 ; VII, 140, 316, 318.
8. This view of the *Iliad* as a document of material and moral simplicity was a popular
development in Homeric criticism in the last part of the eighteenth and the first part of
the nineteenth centuries. Its existence as a critical theory does not minimize its reality
for individuals. Theories of criticism are facts in the experience of many men before they
are literary theories ; and when they cease to be real for humanity they cease to be valid
theories. That Thoreau was aware of this critical theory is evident from his comments
in *Writings*, IX, 244–5, in which, acknowledging the simplicity of the age which Homer
depicts, he suggests that this simplicity was not necessarily characteristic of the age in
which Homer lived, or at least, of the life that the poet led. He surmised that Homer was
describing not the life that he knew but the life that he yearned for, and he identified
himself with Homer in this respect : "That reader who most fully appreciates the poet
and derives the greatest pleasure from his works himself lives in circumstances most like
those of the poet himself."

learned the lesson that most have yet to learn: that the things of the gods are not understandable by mortals.[9]

In the light of Homer's humanity Thoreau could lay down his burden of aspiration and regard the different aspects of his nature as equally good. He could say without any feeling of contradiction, "I find an instinct in me conducting to a mystic spiritual life, and also another to a primitive savage life."[1] This wildness, which would certainly bewilder and shame a conventionally religious or aesthetically philosophical man, did not disturb Thoreau at all. He even spoke of it with pride.[2] It was a proof to him of his connection with the men of an earlier time, possible evidence of recapitulation.[3] The wildness of his own nature was only a part of the wildness and savagery of universal nature. This savagery he recognized; at times it appealed to him, at other times it repelled him in spite of his efforts not to be repelled. But he accepted it as Homer accepted his world, as something that was and for which there was probably somewhere an adequate and innocent explanation.[4]

As Thoreau alternated between the spiritual and the primitive, so on a more commonplace level he alternated between the active and the contemplative: "Now I am Alexander, and then I am Homer."[5] Activity had a special meaning for him, removed from any suggestion of business or commerce. It meant hoeing beans, picking berries, chopping wood; and in that light he found it one of the great satisfactions and realities of life. He admired the plain laboring man, the woodchopper, whether Homer's or his own Therien, who also admired Homer. He urged the scholar to manual labor as a way of putting reality into his life and works.[6]

But he could also sit for hours rapt in revery, "What, after all, does the practicalness of life amount to? The things immediate to be done are very trivial. . . . I could postpone them all to hear this locust

9. This whole philosophy seems to me epitomized in the classical snow-vision in Thomas Mann's *The Magic Mountain*.

1. *Writings*, VII, 384; journal of August 23, 1845; in expanded form in *ibid.*, II, 232.

2. *Ibid.*, V, 225; VI, 36; VII, 256, 296; VIII, 171.

3. *Ibid.*, II, *Walden*, "Higher Laws," *passim;* I, 21, 237.

4. Once he failed to bring himself to eat the squirrels he had killed, but again he persisted in killing, broiling, and eating a bird in order to "fulfill fate, and so at length, perhaps, detect the secret innocence of these incessant tragedies which Heaven allows." (*Ibid.*, I, 236–7.) And he achieved a masterpiece of optimistic acceptance in these words: "I love to see that Nature is so rife with life that myriads can be afforded to be sacrificed and suffered to prey on one another: that tender organizations can be so serenely squashed out of existence like pulp,—tadpoles which herons gobble up, and tortoises and toads run over in the road; and that sometimes it has rained flesh and blood! . . . The impression made on a wise man is that of universal innocence. Poison is not poisonous after all, nor are any wounds fatal."

5. *Ibid.*, VII, 345.

6. *Ibid.*, I, 108–11, *passim.* For an amusing illustration of this point of view see *ibid.*, XX, 295; journal of December 26, 1860.

sing."[7] In the eight years between Harvard and Walden Thoreau had preferred now contemplation, now action. At Walden he seemed to incline again toward the contemplative.[8] But it was no longer necessary for him to choose between the active and the contemplative, between the primitive and the spiritual; he meant to live henceforth a life natural and human, behaving well according to his view of good behavior,[9] not grieving overmuch for his errors, accepting what revelation might come, freeing his life from the impedimenta which might hinder that revelation but making no effort to force it.

So he realized at Walden Homeric simplicity both of life and of thought. He had achieved his release from one kind of life into another; he was living the *Iliad*. He could hardly believe in his material freedom; he derived an almost childish pleasure from it. He had to remind himself that he was really free, answerable to no one, free to come and go as he chose, eat when he felt like it, stay out late at night, roam far afield: "Shall I go down this long hill in the rain to fish in the pond? I ask myself. And I say to myself: Yes, roam far, grasp life and conquer it, learn much and live. Your fetters are knocked off; you are really free. Stay till late in the night; be unwise and daring."[1] With the material freedom came free time for his investigation. He rejoiced in the solitude and silence.[2] He lived "nearer to those parts of the universe and to those eras in history which had most attracted" him.[3]

He did not use his freedom for much reading, even in his favorite eras in history. Yet he did add something to the scope of his classical reading, exploring the first book of Ovid's *Metamorphoses*. The first quotation from Ovid appeared on the frontispiece of *The Week*, lines appropriate for that position because they described the creation of rivers.[4] Other quotations from Ovid were used later in *The Week* for comparison with and explanation of current phenomena: mortals were hard because they sprang from stones,[5] the coming of spring was like the creation of cosmos from chaos,[6] an upturned scow on the shore revealed the history of

7. *Ibid.*, I, 145. See also *ibid.*, II, 123.

8. *Ibid.*, I, 142-3. Perhaps the most significant indication of change is in *ibid.*, I, 229-30, where Thoreau took that portion of the journal (*ibid.*, VII, 172-3; January 23, 1841) in which he had once expressed his approbation of the routine of daily chores and his satisfaction that the great issues of life should be subordinated to barn-shingling, changed "routine" to the routine of sunshine and fine days, and withdrew his approbation of the elevation of the immediate above the ultimate. His employment of the same phrases in a passage of opposite meaning would seem to indicate a definite change of feeling.

9. *Ibid.*, II, 11; VIII, 137.

1. *Ibid.*, VII, 385; journal of August 23, 1845. See also *ibid.*, II, 230-1.

2. *Ibid.*, VII, 381.

3. *Ibid.*, II, 97. This seems additional evidence of the theory that he was living the Homeric life.

4. Ovid, *Metamorphoses* i, 39-42. For this and other quotations from Ovid see App. B, "Ovid."

5. *Writings*, II, 6.

6. *Ibid.*, II, 346.

commerce.[7] Thoreau made no comment on Ovid as a poet or on the *Metamorphoses* as poetry;[8] he was apparently interested only in the myth and especially in the myth of the creation, the beginning of things.

Ovid was Thoreau's only new classical discovery of the period.[9] Most of the classical quotations in *The Week* and *Walden* were simply repetitions from earlier writing. This was true of the Pythagorean selections and of most of the miscellaneous and isolated quotation. The early essays on and translations of Persius and Anacreon were included in *The Week* as literary interludes without additional quotation or comment. Two of Pindar's fables also appeared in *The Week,* stories of the origins of Thera and Rhodes.[1] Of Pindar himself Thoreau had nothing new to say; again his interest seemed to be in mythological origins. Horace Thoreau neither discussed nor quoted. He continued to read and to comment on Vergil,[2] repeating his appreciation of the poet's proof of the sameness and continuity of things[3] and mentioning him with Aeschylus and Homer.[4] There was no new quotation from Aeschylus, but Thoreau again expressed admiration for the quality of his verse[5] and appeared to place him among the poets and close to Homer.

Homer he carried to Walden and kept on his table, apparently both in Greek, to the gratification of the woodchopper Therien,[6] and in Pope's English translation, to the gratification of some thief.[7a] By his own confession Thoreau read little in the book, but that did not mean that he had ceased to value it. He was living the *Iliad* now and had no need to read it. Nor did the fact that he read less in other books prove that he valued books less. Never did he give more emphatic and enthusiastic utterance to his regard for books and for Homer. It was during the Walden period that he produced the bulk of his general literary criticism.

While admitting that everything that was printed and bound was not

7. *Ibid.,* I, 228.

8. Later quotations from Ovid (*Writings,* VIII, 144–5) were accompanied by comment on Greek mythology and the Greek language but by no comment on Ovid or the quality of his poetry.

9. In *The Week* and *Walden* there appeared for the first time traces of reading in Cato and Varro, but the journals of the Walden years show no sign of this. In the journal (*Writings,* VII, 430) Thoreau gives a description of his bread-making at Walden, without any mention of Cato. In *Walden* (*Writings,* II, 70) much the same account appears, but now Cato's recipe has been added. This would suggest that the Cato recipe is from later reading. So far as we know, Thoreau had no access to the husbandry writers until 1851. (See App. A, No. 47.)

1. *Writings,* I, 258–9. See *ibid.,* V, 375–92, for a larger group of selections from Pindar. The story of the origin of Rhodes is in this group; that of the origin of Thera is not.

2. See App. B, "Vergil," for quotations.   3. *Writings,* I, 93.

4. *Ibid.,* II, 115.   5. *Ibid.,* VII, 464.

6. *Ibid.,* VII, 365–6; July, 1845. Thoreau read Therien a passage from the *Iliad* XVI (see App. B, "Homer"); in the *Huntington Journal Fragments* (*HM 13182*) there is additional translation from the same book.

7a. See *Writings* II, 191, and Supplement to App. A, No. 10.

a book[8] and asserting that many books of little worth were written almost by a manufacturing process, still he maintained that in all books there was some echo at least of the best in literature. Statistics, fiction, news, reports, and periodicals he placed in the lower brackets. Science and natural history he found too factual and statistical.[9] History was both too factual and too ancient; it should be biography, the record of men, not of facts; and biography should be autobiography, man's experience made personal.[1] History was really only a prose narrative of poetic deeds; history, exaggerated, became poetry and truth "referred to a new standard."[2]

For Thoreau was inclined to believe that the only literature really worth reading was great poetry, "the last and finest result" of thought and wisdom and yet "a natural fruit."[3] When he spoke of great poetry the *Iliad* was his archetype, and when he spoke of the poet his archetype was Homer. He had much to say of Homer in *The Week*. In his general comments he emphasized the timelessness of the *Iliad*.

There are few books which are fit to be remembered in our wisest hours, but the Iliad is brightest in the serenest days, and embodies still all the sunlight that fell on Asia Minor. No modern joy or ecstasy of ours can lower its height or dim its lustre, but there it lies in the east of literature, as it were the earliest and latest production of the human mind.[4]

If in his general comments Thoreau spoke of the timelessness of Homer, in his more specific comments and in single references and quotations it was the poet's accuracy to nature that he seemed to admire most. Thoreau believed a true account of the actual to be the best poetry;[5] he wanted nothing omitted, nothing added, nothing minimized or exaggerated. Homer satisfied him in this respect: "It is enough if Homer but say the sun sets. He is as serene as nature, and we can hardly detect the enthusiasm of the bard. It is as if nature spoke."[6]

The selections from Homer which Thoreau quoted or referred to presented no thought.[7] Hector advancing to the fore and retreating to the rear of battle like the moon alternately emerging from and disappearing behind the clouds, the woodcutter spreading his morning meal, the night watch of the Trojans, Juno going down the Idaean mountains, Nestor's account of the march of the Pylians, all these were scenes,

8. Material in this paragraph not documented is summarized from *Writings*, I, 93–9.
9. *Ibid.*, I, 100, 386 ff.   1. *Ibid.*, I, 161–3.
2. *Ibid.*, VII, 412; 1845–47.   3. *Ibid.*, I, 93–4.
4. *Ibid.*, I, 97, 394. For the timelessness of truth without specific application to the *Iliad* see *ibid.*, I, 160–1.
5. *Ibid.*, I, 347.   6. *Ibid.*, I, 94.
7. For these quotations see *ibid.*, I, 95–6, and App. B, "Homer."

full, satisfying, slow-moving, majestic scenes. They contained a great deal of nature in the restricted and descriptive sense, and they proved to Thoreau that his world was Homer's world. As the timelessness of Homer was proof of the historical continuity of man, his naturalness was an indication of the universal sameness of nature.

Most of the actual literary criticism comes from *The Week;* in *Walden,* where Thoreau was advertising a way to better living, he used a different approach. He was not reporting accumulated conviction on specific points; he was saying, "Come, follow me." He offered no criticism of Homer for those who had never read Homer, but he uttered a plea to his readers to try the classics. He was the learned man speaking to the unlearned. He was the educated man answering the professional educator, the proponent of "practical" education. The arguments came from him with a special conviction since he did not make his living from teaching the classics, since he was dissatisfied with many of the conservative tendencies in the established educational system,[8] and since he was not even interested in such general projects as the preservation of the humanities. They were, however, much the same arguments that are in use today.

In the first place, he believed that the classics were the best in literature, the highest achievement from an artistic point of view, "works as refined, as solidly done, and as beautiful almost as the morning itself; for later writers, say what we will of their genius, have rarely, if ever, equalled the elaborate beauty and finish and the lifelong and heroic literary labors of the ancients."[9] There was a touch of indignation in his next comment: "They only talk of forgetting them who never knew them. It will be soon enough to forget them when we have the learning and the genius which will enable us to attend to and appreciate them."[1] The same indignation tinged his response to the accusation that they were old and impractical. As for the fact that they were old, "We might as well omit to study Nature because she is old."[2] Thoreau would have found John King's wonder that a man could love both Homer and nature utterly incomprehensible. Homer was the best representation of nature that Thoreau knew, a transcript of nature three thousand years ago. And contemporary civilization, on the other hand, was the only modern transcript of the *Iliad.*[3] Homer and nature represented the same life, continuous, unchanging, identical. Where true values were concerned there was no time: ". . . these works of art have such an immortality as the works of nature and are modern at the same time that they are ancient, like the sun and stars, and occupy by right no small

8. *Writings*, VIII, 83; X, 287; XIX, 67–8.
9. *Ibid.*, II, 115. See also *ibid.*, VII, 371.   1. *Ibid.*, II, 115.
2. *Ibid.*, II, 112.   3. *Ibid.*, II, 115.

share of the present."[4] If time was at all to be considered it added value to a work, for survival was a proof of worth.[5]

As to their alleged impracticality, the classics constituted the "noblest recorded thoughts of men," the "treasured wealth of the world and the fit inheritance of generations and nations." They confirmed the experience of the individual. Not to know them was to have "a very imperfect knowledge of the history of the human race."[6]

Thoreau not only found the classics artistically and practically valuable but admired the intellectual effort which it took to read them and approved their disciplinary value. He felt that it required a strenuous exercise of "wisdom and valor and generosity" to read Homer and Aeschylus.[7] This is the reverse side of the theory that the reader takes from the printed page what he puts into it; in the case of such men as Homer and Aeschylus the reader must exert himself to be equal to taking from the page what the poet has put there. Not everyone can read the great works of literature.

He insisted, too, that the works should be read in the language in which they were written and that a knowledge of the Greek and Latin tongues was essential for the understanding of the real and vital meanings of words: "It is worth the expense of youthful days and costly hours, if you learn only some words of an ancient language, which are raised out of the trivialness of the street, to be perpetual suggestions and provocations."[8] This was from the man who said that the cost of a thing was the amount of life that had to be exchanged for it.

Thoreau's tremendous admiration for Greek poetry came from his often repeated conviction that it was a channel of revelation. The revelation was present both in its substance, myth, and in its expression, music. In the earlier journals Thoreau had worked out his theory of sphere music and had moved steadily toward the idea that myth con-

---

4. *Ibid.*, VII, 371. See also *ibid.*, VII, 376: "Three thousand years are not agone; they are still lingering here this summer morn." See also *ibid.*, I, 163–4: "What is near to the heart of this generation is fair and bright still. Greece lies outspread fair and sunshiny in floods of light, for there is the sun and daylight in her literature and art."

5. *Ibid.*, II, 114: "Two thousand summers have imparted to the monuments of Grecian literature, as to her marbles, only a maturer golden and autumnal tint." Also *ibid.*, I, 402, of old books: "The true finish is the work of time, and the use to which a thing is put."

6. *Ibid.*, II, 112–20, *passim*.

7. *Ibid.*, II, 111. For a similar statement see *ibid.*, VII, 377.

8. *Ibid.*, II, 111–12. See also *ibid.*, VIII, 143, on the "elegant terseness and conciseness" of the Latin language. Thoreau's interest in philology was philosophic and poetic. He approved the German philological studies because they indirectly served the cause of philosophy and poetry (*ibid.*, I, 148). He was always concerned wtih the roots of words. He enjoyed connecting "ligature" and "religion," defining a house as a *sedes* or "seat" and a "community" as a league for mutual defense, making distinctions between *lacus*, *amnis*, *rivus*, and *fluvius*. He liked such half-coined and new-applied expressions as "antepenultimate hours." Borrowings from the Latin, *tintinnabulum, exuviae, scoriae, agricola laboriosus*, dotted his writing. His extensive word experiments were the lobe-lip-leaf nightmare of *Walden* (*ibid.*, II, 337–40), the wild apple essay (*ibid.*, V, 316–17; VIII, 222), and the Latin *nox* fantasy (*ibid.*, IX, 272–3).

tained the substance of truth. At Walden he gave that idea positive statement. Myths were "vestiges of ancient poems, wrecks of poems."[9] They
preceded literature and poetry.[1] They were an approach to a universal
language and "proof of a common humanity"; they contained "only enduring and essential truth, the I and you, the here and there, the now
and then, being omitted."[2]

He had found somewhere a curious book, *Mystagogus Poeticus, Or
The Muses Interpreter* by Alexander Ross, a kind of classical dictionary
of mythology, each story followed by an interpretation or a number of
possible interpretations.[3] He used this book to work out a detailed development of the general theory. Groups of the myths were listed in the
journal and in *The Week,* and a few isolated stories appeared elsewhere
in his writings. Some he mentioned by name only,[4] for others he related
the stories, for a few he added explanation and comment. Among those
which received more than casual listing were the stories of Aristaeus;[5]
of Aeacus, Minos, and Rhadamanthus;[6] of Bacchus' driving the Tyrrhenian mariners mad;[7] of Momus' objection to the house of Minerva;[8] of
the *pius* Aeneas carrying his father on his back;[9a] of Antaeus;[1a] of Amphion, Marysas, and Thamyris and the origin of music;[2a] and of Apollo
and Admetus.

The story of Apollo and Admetus was his favorite; he referred to it
innumerable times; it illustrated his own tragedy in being forced to serve
the god of business.[3a] Others had less personal applications, but most of
them fit easily into Thoreau's thought; even when he gave no definite
interpretation, either his own or that of Ross, it is usually possible to see
why Thoreau found a myth instructive. But he did not think it necessary
for a myth to have any special application; he found in mythology "ma-

---

9. *Ibid.,* I, 164.

2. *Ibid.,* I, 59, 60.

1. *Ibid.,* II, 340; XII, 109.

3. For description see App. A, No. 46.

4. *Writings,* I, 58–9; Narcissus, Endymion, Memnon, Phaëthon, the Sirens, Pan,
Prometheus, the Sphinx, the Sibyls, the Eumenides, the Parcae, the Graces, the Muses,
Nemesis.

5. *Ibid.,* I, 57–8; VII, 394; Alexander Ross, pp. 29–31.

6. There are two stories narrated in this connection: one, that people must go naked
to Hades (*Writings,* VII, 392), and the other, the story of Aeacus' turning the people
of Aegina into ants (*ibid.,* I, 58; VII, 392). The second story is also referred to in *ibid.,* II,
101. Both stories are in Ross, *op. cit.,* pp. 8–9.

7. *Writings,* I, 58; VII, 393; Ross, p. 41.   8. *Writings,* II, 37; Ross, p. 293.

9a. *Writings,* I, 136; VII, 392; Ross, pp. 11–13.

1a. *Writings,* VII, 393; Ross, pp. 19–20.

2a. *Writings,* VII, 392–3; Ross, pp. 17–18 (all under Amphion).

3a. *Writings,* VII, 391; Ross, p. 23 (under Apollo). Although Thoreau lists this
myth with others taken from Ross, Ross does not interpret it as Thoreau did. Thoreau
had referred to the myth many times before he became acquainted with the interpretations of Ross. He might have found the myth in any number of places. Marble, *Thoreau,
His Home, Friends and Books,* p. 98, says that he found it in Euripides, but does not give
her authority for the statement. The story is in the *Alcestis* which Thoreau read at
Harvard.

terials and hints for a history of the rise and progress of the race."[4] He
was in favor of multiple interpretation and many surmises:

The hidden significance of these fables which is sometimes thought to have
been detected, the ethics running parallel to the poetry and history, are not
so remarkable as the readiness with which they may be made to express a
variety of truths. As if they were the skeletons of still older and more universal
truths than any whose flesh and blood they are for the time made to wear. It
is like striving to make the sun, or the wind, or the sea symbols to signify
exclusively the particular thoughts of our day. But what signifies it?[5]

Of Bacchus and the Tyrrhenian mariners he said, ". . . we are not
concerned about the historical truth of this, but rather a higher poetical
truth. We seem to hear the music of a thought, and care not if the understanding be not gratified."[6] He finally abandoned the words for the
music: "The expressions of the poet cannot be analyzed. . . . There are
indeed no *words* quite worthy to be set to his music. But what matter if
we do not hear the words always, if we hear the music?"[7] He came at last
to his ultimate definition of poetry: "Poetry is the mysticism of mankind."[8]

It was not of the intellect but of the sense, not of reason but of ecstasy.
It went far beyond the printed page;[9] it dwelt partially in sound;[1] it
culminated simply in sensation:

I see, smell, taste, hear, feel, that everlasting Something to which we are
allied, at once our maker, our abode, our destiny, our very Selves; the one
historic truth . . . the actual glory of the universe . . . I have seen how
the foundations of the world are laid, and I have not the least doubt that it
will stand a good while.[2]

He felt faint intimations of revelation,[3] glimpses of reality, of things in
their eternal relations.[4a]

4. *Writings*, I, 165.
5. *Ibid.*, I, 61; with slight variation, VII, 392.
6. *Ibid.*, I, 58; VII, 393.
7. *Ibid.*, I, 350. See also *ibid.*: "It is only by a miracle that poetry is written at all.
It is not recoverable thought, but a hue caught from a vaster receding thought"; and
ibid., I, 400: "A true poem is distinguished not so much by a felicitous expression, or any
thought it suggests, as by the atmosphere which surrounds it."
8. *Ibid.*, I, 350.
9. *Ibid.*, II, 123: "But while we are confined to books . . . we are in danger of forgetting the language which all things and events speak without metaphor, which alone
is copious and standard. . . . Will you be a reader, a student merely, or a seer?" See also
ibid., VII, 396.
1. *Ibid.*, I, 181–4.
2. *Ibid.*, I, 182. See also *ibid.*, VII, 365; July 14, 1845; and II, 145–6: "Sometimes, when
I compare myself with other men, methinks I am favored by the gods. They seem to
whisper joy to me beyond my deserts, and that I do have a solid warrant and surety at
their hands, which my fellows do not. . . . I am especially guided and guarded."
3. *Ibid.*, I, 310.   4a. *Ibid.*, I, 383.

What the intimations and the realities were it was hard to put into words. "The true harvest of my daily life," he said, "is somewhat as intangible and indescribable as the tints of morning or evening."[5] "Can you put mysteries into words? Do you presume to fable of the ineffable?"[6] He related the story from Sadi of the man in the rose garden of revery who, recalled to the world and asked by his friends what he had brought them from his dreams, answered: ". . . I fancied to myself and said, when I can reach the rose-bower, I will fill my lap with flowers, and bring them as a present to my friends; but when I got there, the fragrance of the roses so intoxicated me, that the skirt dropped from my hands."[17]

In the chapter in *Walden* called "Higher Laws" Thoreau endeavored to bring back some roses. But the chapter is disappointing. Although he was able to state a very simple rule for the discovery of laws,[8] he was unable to discover many. He came to the not unusual conclusion that all forms of sensuality should be avoided, in particular the sensuality of eating animal food.[9] The published statement in *Walden* was an expansion in form and a limitation in thought of the query in the journal: "What if we were to obey these fine dictates, these divine suggestions, which are addressed to the mind and not to the body, which are certainly true, —not to eat meat, not to buy, or sell, or barter, etc., etc., etc.?"[1] One cannot feel much confidence in these higher laws. A man with a divine message is not likely to write it "etc., etc., etc." But Thoreau had spent eight years waiting and listening for a message. He felt obliged to make a report and he did the best he could.

He was on much surer ground when he retreated to generalities and to convictions of sense rather than of the reason. He was, as he had always been, certain of the existence of "the other world"; he had made, usually under sensory stimulus, excursions into a supersensory world;

---

5. *Ibid.*, II, 239.
6. *Ibid.*, I, 71. See also *ibid.*, I, 145–6: "The most glorious fact in my experience is not anything that I have done or may hope to do, but a transient thought, or vision, or dream, which I have had. I would give all the wealth of the world . . . for one true vision."
7. *Ibid.*, I, 80.
8. *Ibid.*, I, 387–8: "The process of discovery is very simple. An unwearied and systematic application of known laws to nature causes the unknown to reveal themselves." This is in a discussion of the general superiority of poetry to science.
9. This brings us to the question of how far Porphyry may have influenced Thoreau. That they reached the same conclusion seems to be about all that they had in common. Porphyry's arguments are too interlinked with philosophical system to appeal to Thoreau. Thoreau objected to animal food on the grounds that it was distasteful to prepare, that killing animals was a callous infliction of pain, and that it was better for an intellectual not to eat much of any food. He had given up hunting; he considered giving up fishing. But he had no foolish scruples; he had often fished because he needed the food, and he thought that he could eat a fried rat with relish if it were necessary (*Writings*, II, 240). It would perhaps be unfair to say that he was not at all influenced by Porphyry, but the influence seems to have come through Alcott rather than through Porphyry.
1. *Writings*, VII, 382; journal of August 15, 1845.

he considered whether it might not be through the development of the senses that man would finally inhabit that world.

But there is only necessary a moment's sanity and sound sense, to teach us that there is a nature behind the ordinary, in which we have only some vague preemption right and western reserve as yet. We live on the outskirts of that region. . . . Our present senses are but rudiments of what they are destined to become. We are comparatively deaf and dumb and blind, and without smell or taste or feeling. . . . The ears were made . . . to hear celestial sounds. The eyes . . . to behold beauty now invisible. May we not *see* God? . . . Is not Nature rightly read, that of which she is commonly taken to be the symbol merely? . . . I am not without hope that we may, even here and now, obtain some accurate information concerning that OTHER WORLD which the instinct of mankind has so long predicted.[2]

What he could give his readers in *Walden* was suggestive only.

I learned this, at least, by my experiment; that if one advances confidently in the direction of his dreams, and endeavors to live the life which he has imagined, he will meet with a success unexpected in common hours. He will put some things behind, will pass an invisible boundary; new, universal, and more liberal laws will begin to establish themselves around and within him. . . . In proportion as he simplifies his life, the laws of the universe will appear less complex, and solitude will not be solitude, nor poverty poverty, nor weakness weakness.[3]

We should expect this rather matter-of-fact account in *Walden;* the journal passages are much more extravagantly written. He speaks of dying to the old life, of being translated, of walking on water, of stepping forth onto the clouds.[4]

His experiment had been successful. He had "put some things behind": the sorrow for John's death; the futility of surface living in the years that followed; the conflict between the poet and society, Apollo's drudgery for Admetus. If one source of revelation had failed and nature had been imperturbably uncommunicative of secrets,[5] he had on the other hand met an unexpected success in the renewal and extension of mystic experience.

There are certainly realities which are not material. They are purely personal; they cannot be transferred from one to another; they cannot be judged by any other than the one who experiences them. Such a reality is death; all men believe it to be a fact; no man alive knows it as a fact. Such a reality for Thoreau was his other world; he had always believed it to be a fact; now he had had recurrent knowledge of it as fact, however little "accurate information" he might be able to transmit concerning it.

2. *Ibid.*, I, 408–12, *passim.* See entire section, *ibid.*, I, 407–13.
3. *Ibid.*, II, 356.   4. This is in the *Huntington Journal Fragments* (*HM13182*).
5. *Writings*, II, 312, 354.

A great optimism is one of the marks of the mystic, and Thoreau's persistent optimism is an indication that he did experience that of which he spoke. The documents of the Walden years read in their confidence and enthusiasm much like the journal of the good year of 1838; there is indeed a curious parallelism between these two periods. In 1838 Thoreau was reading the *Iliad;* he was recording mystic experience; he summarized his life and his philosophy in the essay "Sound and Silence." At Walden the *Iliad* seemed always in his mind; he again knew mystic ecstasy; and he actually closed *The Week* with a part of the same essay:

Silence is audible to all men, at all times, and in all places. She is when we hear inwardly, sound when we hear outwardly. . . . She is Truth's speaking-trumpet . . . the Grecian or silent and melodious era is ever sounding and resounding in the ears of men. . . . A good book is the plectrum with which our else silent lyres are struck. . . . It were vain for me to endeavor to interpret the Silence. She cannot be done into English. . . . Nevertheless, we will go on. . . .[6]

Thoreau had come full circle. In the ten years between 1837–47 he had tried in turn all the transcendental avenues to truth: contemplation of self, study of books, investigation of the world, both of men and of nature. Now at last he came back to the starting place. Reaffirming his original belief that the answer must lie within himself, he could afford to relinquish the special environment of the past two years. On September 6, 1847, he left Walden.

6. *Writings,* I, 418–20. This essay and particularly the condensation of it appearing in *The Week* is a peculiar combination of the mystic and the practical. Thoreau's determination to fit his statements concerning the Grecian Era and a good book into a context where they seem almost awkward is an indication of the importance which he attached to them.

IV

Lost Youth

"The period of youth is past. . . . It is a season of . . . small fruits and trivial experiences. . . . But there is an aftermath . . . and some spring flowers bloom again . . ."

THOREAU left Walden restored and confident. But just as his life there had seemed to parallel the happy year of 1838, so did the post-Walden period parallel the years which followed 1838. The external circumstances were similar in many ways: both periods involved residence at Emerson's and consequent loss in private living; during both Thoreau sustained personal bereavement, John's death in 1842 and the death of his sister Helen in 1849;[1] during both he was beset by the problem of making a living and forced into activities not entirely agreeable to him, surveying, lecturing, writing for publication; both times too he was troubled by unsatisfactory relationships with certain of his friends;[2] and this time, as before, the journal was for long intervals either negligently kept or systematically destroyed, so that it is difficult to follow him closely.[3]

The absence of the journal suggests a parallelism of mental state as well as of exterior circumstance, and the glimpses we are able to catch of Thoreau confirm this impression. In "Ktaadn," published in 1848, there are disquieting indications of restlessness and confusion. Thoreau was ready and waiting, but the gods did not speak. He stood on the bank of the river watching logs caught in a jam and read there his own story: "Methinks that must be where all my property lies, cast up on the rocks on some distant and unexplored stream, and waiting for an unheard-of freshet to fetch it down. O make haste, ye gods, with your winds and rains, and start the jam before it rots!"[4]

1. There is little indication in the journals that Helen's death affected him deeply. An entry of December 24, 1850 (*Writings*, VIII, 130), may involve reference to it, and there are entries in the *Huntington Journal Fragments* (*HM13182*) which refer to the death of a beloved one as not constituting separation.

2. The "Love and Friendship" theme of a decade ago again appears in the journals. Although in the published journal the masculine gender is used in all Thoreau's remarks on friendship, both genders appear in the discarded *Huntington Journal Fragments*. It would require careful study to determine whether the gender shift is accidental or deliberate, and if it is deliberate whether it is intended as a disguise or for purposes of distinction. It seems almost certain, however, that Thoreau felt embarrassment in his friendship with Emerson and some kind of emotional involvement with Lidian Emerson.

3. See above, p. 44, n. 7.   4. *Writings*, III, 58; "Ktaadn."

Thoreau had often been impatient at the slowness of revelation, but he had never yet entertained the idea that there was no revelation or that when it came it might be other than glorious. Now, standing on the Burnt Lands, he felt uncertainty and fear.

This was that Earth of which we have heard, made out of Chaos and Old Night. . . . Man was not to be associated with it. It was Matter, vast, terrific,—not his Mother Earth that we have heard of . . . What is it to be admitted to a museum . . . compared with being shown some star's surface, some hard matter in its home! I stand in awe of my body, this matter to which I am bound has become so strange to me. I fear not spirits, ghosts, of which I am one . . . but I fear bodies, I tremble to meet them. What is this Titan that has possession of me? Talk of mysteries! Think of our life in nature,—daily to be shown matter, to come in contact with it,—rocks, trees, wind on our cheeks! the *solid* earth! the *actual* world! the *common sense! Contact! Contact! Who* are we? *Where* are we?[5]

Once before, at John's death, Thoreau had been unable to ignore a material fact or to clothe it in transcendental theory. Now again the actual was suddenly too immediate for denial. Nature was no longer a half-transparent veil through which he glimpsed the other world; it was a harsh, impenetrable barrier and the other world had disappeared.

Thoreau's state of mind was reflected in changes in his habits and attitudes. He did not read much in the classics, and he began to take an interest in contemporary matters. He could not, of course, remove the classics from his thoughts simply by ceasing to read nor could he in his contemporary interests ignore their classical bases and parallels. In "Ktaadn," for example, there is no sign of classical reading but there is the usual sprinkling of classical vocabulary and allusion. Most of the allusions are of one type, specific modern applications of ancient myth. Thoreau seemed to have given up reading mythology and history in favor of discovering them: "Why read history, then, if the ages and the generations are now?"[6] In the mountain streams the fish with their changing colors and slippery evasions reminded him of Proteus;[7] he remarked the realization of the fabled hostility of sheep and wolves;[8] shooting the rapids recalled the story of the Argo passing through the Symplegades;[9] the mountains awakened recollections of the "old epic and dramatic poets, of Atlas, Vulcan, the Cyclops, and Prometheus. Such was Caucasus and the rock where Prometheus was bound. Aeschylus had no doubt visited such scenery as this."[1]

In 1849 Thoreau published his essay "Civil Disobedience," a very

5. *Ibid.*, III, 78–9; "Ktaadn."   6. *Ibid.*, III, 87; "Ktaadn."
7. *Ibid.*, III, 59; "Ktaadn."
8. *Ibid.*, III, 32; "Ktaadn"; this is probably a reflection of Aesop.
9. *Ibid.*, III, 35; "Ktaadn"; this is probably an echo of Orpheus.
1. *Ibid.*, III, 70; "Ktaadn."

strong sign of concern with practical, contemporary problems. Yet the thesis of "Civil Disobedience" is firmly based on Sophocles' *Antigone*, and it seems fairly certain that Thoreau reread the play at this time for he quoted from it in *The Week* two passages which illustrate the thought of the essay; one the dialogue between Antigone and her weak sister Ismene who dared not disobey the law, and the other the conversation between Creon and Antigone in which she maintained the superiority of divine decrees to the laws of men.[2]

But probably the greatest change in Thoreau's habits was in his method of keeping the journal. When the long-interrupted record began again in 1850 it was not much like its earlier self. For the first year, it is true, Thoreau followed his old practice of revising, deleting, and condensing, but this was a matter of form only; he made no attempt at synthesis of thought. With 1851 he abandoned any attempt at organization even of form. The journal became predominately a report of the minutiae of the changing seasons at Concord, supplemented by the personal and local anecdote so rigorously excluded heretofore, illustrated by mythological and historical analogies, and punctuated by increasingly long and frequent botanical and ornithological lists. His reading was no longer assimilated into his writing but appeared in notes and transcriptions, complete with source and page references. He developed a counting and dating tendency: twenty swallows' nests under the barn eaves, thirty-eight lighthouses in Massachusetts, thirteen partridge eggs on June 4, the first peculiar summer breathing of frogs on June 5. Thoreau had advised his readers in *Walden*, "It is not worth the while to go round the world to count the cats in Zanzibar. Yet do this even till you can do better,"[3] and he seemed indeed to be counting cats in Zanzibar. "Let me not be in haste to detect the *universal law*," he said, "let me see more clearly a particular instance of it!"[4]

The particular instances were vague and sometimes contradictory. He could not distinguish whim and superstition from divine admonition.[5] He came to one decision after another on the relative importance of nature and man. At one time nature must be "viewed humanly to be viewed at all";[6] however wonderful nature may be, "the standing miracle to man is man."[7] Now he resolves to devote himself to friends and neighbors; that will be better than "a wild walk."[8] Still he has to force himself to try to enjoy men "as animals, at least."[9] At one time it

2. *Ibid.*, I, 140.   3. *Ibid.*, II, 354.
4. *Ibid.*, IX, 157; journal of December 25, 1851.
5. *Ibid.*, VIII, 143; journal of January 10, 1851; *ibid.*, VIII, 380; journal of August 8, 1851; *ibid.*, IX, 136; journal of December 13, 1851.
6. *Ibid.*, X, 163; June 30, 1852.
7. *Ibid.*, VIII, 207. This may come from Young's *Night Thoughts,* Bk. I, l. 84.
8. *Ibid.*, IX, 184–5; January 12, 1852.
9. *Ibid.*, VIII, 421; August 23, 1851.

is communion with nature that makes a man healthy and cheerful;[1] at another, nature simply reflects man's physical and moral state.[2]

The journal not only reflects in its changed character the state of Thoreau's mind but also illustrates the other changes already noted in Thoreau. His classicism follows the pattern of the two preceding years: much lingering flavor, little current reading, and another extension of his theory of myth. To 1850 belong two classical imitations which show how much of style and feeling Thoreau had absorbed from his earlier reading; one the description of the beautiful heifer, a prose pastoral of Vergilian flavor and Vergilian excellence,[3] the other the rhapsodic apostrophe to his moon-sister Diana, Orphic in character but lacking the classical restraint and balance that mark even the Orphics.[4]

Thoreau's attempt to read Ovid in 1851 is related to his still-developing theory of myth. He had once enjoyed the first book of the *Metamorphoses* because it told the story of the beginning of things; now he enjoyed the second book because many of its stories purported to explain why things are as they are.[5] Thoreau approved this kind of myth because it was a living thing of which the proof was extant and the principle still in operation, and because it moved from the past to the present which was now Thoreau's direction.

But all this—the quality of the journal, the scanty reading in the classics, the time shift—is circumstantial evidence. When Thoreau speaks of himself in the journal he makes a clear confession. At first there is only the sense of frustration originally expressed in "Ktaadn": "From time to time I overlook the promised land, but I do not feel that I am travelling toward it."[6] "I see somewhat fairer than I enjoy or pos-

1. *Ibid.*, VIII, 193; May 6, 1851; *ibid.*, X, 409–10; November 4, 1852.

2. *Ibid.*, X, 126; June 21, 1852.

3. *Ibid.*, VIII, 67–8; September, 1850. There is no evidence that Thoreau ever read the Greek pastorals. In any case this is definitely the domesticated Vergilian pastoral. For a sign that Thoreau associated it with Vergil see a similar description (*Writings*, XII, 434; August 12, 1854) accompanied by the comment, "reminded me of some frontispieces to Virgil's Bucolics." Notice in this pastoral the allusion to Io, an echo probably either of Aeschylus or of Ovid.

4. *Ibid.*, VIII, 78; 1850. If this seems unsuccessful as an imitation, it should be noted that it was probably not written primarily as such. In the *Huntington Journal Fragments* (HM13182) an essay, "The Sister," is so similar in content, in tone, and even in phrasing both to the Diana passage and to Thoreau's second letter from New York to Lidian Emerson in 1843 that it seems likely that the essay and the apostrophe to Diana were parts or successive versions of the same piece of writing, an imaginative address to Lidian. The essay is so exaggerated in tone and so incoherent in structure that from the point of view either of emotional privacy or of literary pride it could never have been left where it might come into the public eye; while the final apostrophe to Diana, condensed, polished, and impersonalized, might very well pass as a literary exercise and be left in the journal without explanation or need for it. A part of the essay has been quoted by Canby in his discussion of the relationship between Thoreau and Lidian Emerson (*Thoreau*, pp. 160–1).

5. *Writings*, VIII, 144–5. There is a more extensive translation of the story of Phaëthon in the *Huntington Journal Fragments.*   6. *Writings*, VIII, 47; 1850.

sess."[7] "I feel ripe for something, yet do nothing, can't discover what that thing is. . . . I have lain fallow long enough."[8] More definite is this statement, reminiscent of a similar utterance during the depression of 1842: "When on the higher levels we can remember the lower levels, but when on the lower we cannot remember the higher."[9]

He remembered the higher all too well however. "My imagination," he said, "my love and reverence and admiration, my sense of the miraculous, is not so excited by any event as by the remembrance of my youth."[1] There are many utterances on this theme; with increasing force and clarity he connected the barrenness of his current life with the loss of his youth and of the sharp sense perceptions which had been the source of his mystic ecstasies.

Ah, that life that I have known! How hard it is to remember what is most memorable! . . . I can sometimes recall to mind the quality, the immortality, of my youthful life, but in memory is the only relation to it.[2]

Now perchance many sounds and sights only remind me that they once said something to me, and are so by association interesting. I go forth to be reminded of a previous state of existence, if perchance any memento is to be met with hereabouts.[3]

Thoreau's expressions of personal unhappiness have received less attention than they deserve. They make a very small part of the whole journal; they are minimized by occasional expressions of hope[4] and by the generally cheerful and matter-of-fact quality of the rest of the journal. But Thoreau did not believe in letting his emotion influence his reporting. It was the poet's duty to maintain his serenity. The disease was in Thoreau, not in nature, and he should not allow the darkness of his mind to tinge the colors of nature.[5] What he said of himself was little, and that often parenthetical, but words like these can scarcely be ignored.

Methinks my present experience is nothing; my past experience is all in all. I think that no experience which I have today comes up to, or is comparable with, the experiences of my boyhood. . . . My life was ecstasy. In youth, before I lost any of my senses, I can remember that I was all alive, and inhabited my body with inexpressible satisfaction; both its weariness and its refreshment were sweet to me. This earth was the most glorious musical instrument, and I was audience to all its strains. . . . I said to myself,—I said to others,—"There comes into my mind such an indescribable, infinite, all-absorbing, divine, heavenly pleasure, a sense of elevation and expansion and [I] have had nought to do with it. I perceive that I am dealt with by superior

7. *Ibid.*, VIII, 76; October 31, 1850.   8. *Ibid.*, VIII, 101; November 16, 1850.
9. *Ibid.*, VIII, 33; June 9, 1850.   1. *Ibid.*
2. *Ibid.*, VIII, 237–8; June 11, 1851.   3. *Ibid.*, VIII, 302–3; July 12, 1851.
4. *Ibid.*, VIII, 269, 315, 391; IX, 86, 131; X, 126. Notice how often the shift from despair to hope is recorded in a single passage.
5. *Ibid.*, VIII, 303; IX, 85, 233–4, 236; IV, 344; "Thomas Carlyle and his Works."

powers. . . ." I wondered if a mortal had ever known what I knew. I looked in books for some recognition of a kindred experience, but, strange to say, I found none. . . . With all your science can you tell how it is, and whence it is, that light comes into the soul?[6]

His whole unhappiness was represented in his dream of October 26, 1851, in which he struggled through interminable difficulties, quoted lines of poetry which he did not know when conscious, all dealing with regret, memory, and the past, and woke with the thought that his body was a musical instrument from which he heard the last strain die out. He made an effort to explain the dream:

Last evening . . . though I did not write in my Journal, I remember feeling a fertile regret, and deriving even an inexpressible satisfaction, as it were, from my ability to feel regret, which made that evening richer than those which had preceded it. I heard the last strain or flourish, as I woke, played on my body as the instrument. Such I knew I had been and might be again, and my regret arose from the consciousness how little like a musical instrument my body was now.[7]

He heard less often now the music of the spheres: "I hear the tones of my sister's piano below. It reminds me of strains which once I heard more frequently, when, possessed with the inaudible rhythm, I sought my chamber in the cold and communed with my own thoughts. . . . Now I hear those strains but seldom."[8]

Every change he found in himself he attributed to age. "As we grow older," he asked, "is it not ominous that we have more to write about evening, less about morning?"[9] Whereas formerly he had written of the dawn and the sunrise, there was much of evening and moonlight in the journal now.[1] It was actually as though he could not bear full light: "With the coolness and the mild silvery light, I recover some sanity . . . The intense light of the sun unfits me for meditation . . . I am sobered by the moonlight."[2]

He came to the conclusions that as men grow older they become coarse, grow obedient to nature rather than to spirit, and suffer a lessening of intellectual power.[3] He felt this not only as a man but as a poet: "If thou art a writer, write as if thy time was short . . . The spring will not last forever. These fertile and expanding seasons of thy life . . . shall be fewer and farther between. . . . Why did I not use my eyes when I stood on Pisgah?"[4] "The strains from my muse are as rare now-

6. *Ibid.*, VIII, 306–7; July 16, 1851.   7. *Ibid.*, IX, 82.
8. *Ibid.*, IX, 222; January 24, 1852.
9. *Ibid.*, IX, 320; February 25, 1852. See also *ibid.*, VIII, 315; July 18, 1851.
1. *Ibid.*, VIII, 287, 378, 385, 482–7, 495; IX, 38–9, 265, 354.
2. *Ibid.*, VIII, 372. See also *ibid.*, IX, 7: "Lunacy must be a cold excitement, not such insanity as a torrid sun on the brain would produce."
3. *Ibid.*, VIII, 463; IX, 66, 203–4; X, 417.   4. *Ibid.*, IX, 221. See also *ibid.*, VIII, 330.

adays, or of late years, as the notes of the birds in the winter . . ."[5]

With age too he connected what he felt as his descent from the poetic to the scientific:

I fear that the character of my knowledge is from year to year becoming more distinct and scientific . . . I see details, not wholes nor the shadow of the whole . . .[6]

The poet's second love may be science, not his first,—when use has worn off the bloom. I realize that men may be born to a condition of mind at which others arrive in middle age by the decay of their poetic faculties.[7]

As he associated the life of man with the course of the year and his growth with the plant life of the seasons, he could not hope to recapture his youth, but he could hope for an Indian summer.

In the feelings of the man, too, the year is already past, and he looks forward to the coming winter. His occasional rejuvenescence and faith in the current time is like the aftermath, a scanty crop. . . . The period of youth is past. The year may be in its summer, in its manhood, but it is no longer in the flower of its age. It is a season of withering, of dust and heat, a season of small fruits and trivial experiences. Summer thus answers to manhood. But there is an aftermath in early autumn, and some spring flowers bloom again, followed by an Indian summer of finer atmosphere and of a pensive beauty. May my life be not destitute of its Indian summer, a season of fine and clear, mild weather in which I may prolong my hunting before the winter comes, when I may once more lie on the ground with faith, as in spring, and even with more serene confidence.[8]

The idea of the aftermath comes from Cato's *De re rustica*. Thoreau had reflected in the summer of 1851 that when "our light-and-air seeking tendencies extend too widely for our original root or stem, we must send downward new roots to ally us to the earth."[9] Such a root was his reading in the Roman husbandry writers. He had lived too long with visions and shadows of truth; he needed a solid footing, something connected with his old interests but connected also with activity and routine. Dining with Alcott on August 11, 1851, he took home with him his host's copy of the *Rei rusticae* containing the works of Cato, Varro, Columella, and Palladius.[1] The husbandry writers were not too great a descent from Vergil, the farmer's life was only one step removed from the pastoral; it was man in nature, in Latin literature it was early man in early nature. Thoreau had always regarded farming, when not sub-

---

5. *Ibid.*, IX, 312.　　　　　　6. *Ibid.*, VIII, 406; August 19, 1851.

7. *Ibid.*, IX, 311–12. For other expressions either of this type or on the inadequacy of science see *ibid.*, IX, 378; X, 157–8, 174, 392.

8. *Ibid.*, VIII, 481–2; September 8, 1851. See *ibid.*, XI, 210, for the idea of men and plants whose fruits never ripen.

9. *Ibid.*, VIII, 205.

1. *The Journals of Bronson Alcott*, ed. Shepard, p. 253. See App. A, No. 47.

ordinated to the making of money, as the noblest of occupations, praised by poets and philosophers. All through the fall of 1851 he watched the farmers at their seasonal tasks, cutting the turf, topping the corn, starting the fall plowing. And he read in Cato an account of similar activities, finding in the *De re rustica* repeated proof of the old theory of sameness, affirming it a more genuine history of the people of Rome than the standard Roman histories, and expressing at the same time his approval of the simple life and his own need for a solid footing: "How much the Roman must have been indebted to his agriculture, dealing with the earth, its clods and stubble, its dust and mire. Their farmer consuls were their glory, and they well knew the farm to be the nursery of soldiers. Read Cato to see what kind of legs the Romans stood on."[2] Reading a current farm report in the spring of 1852 he commented, "I feel as if I had got my foot down on to the solid and sunny earth, the basis of all philosophy and poetry, and religion even."[3]

If the Roman and the Concord farmers helped him to get his feet on the ground, there was another combination of the classical and the modern that helped him to lift his head again. His sensitivity to music had been the strongest of his sense perceptions, and it had not wholly deserted him; if he failed to hear the sphere music, he heard and delighted in something which was an audible approximation of it—the sound of the wind in the telegraph wires, the music of the telegraph harp. He insisted that it brought him hope and inspiration and reminded him that there were higher planes of life that he should not forget.[4] He identified it with the Grecian Age and was moved to read the Greek poets: "It intoxicates me. Orpheus is still alive. . . . I do not know but this will make me read the Greek poets."[5] "When I hear the telegraph harp, I think I must read the Greek poets. This sound . . . prophecies finer senses, a finer life, a golden age."[6]

2. *Writings*, VIII, 450. For quotations from Cato see App. B, "Cato." See also *Writings*, VIII, 444–5: "The more we know about the ancients, the more we find that they were like the moderns. . . . Indeed the farmer's was pretty much the same routine then as now." Notice the direction of these comparisons. For references to Cato see App. C.

3. *Writings*, IX, 327. See also *ibid.*, IX, 328, for Thoreau's suggestion that the history of a farm from the natural to the cultivated state would make good matter for an epic and his mention of Vergil's *Eclogues* and *Georgics* and Hesiod's *Works and Days* as parts of such a work. Thoreau once quoted from Hesiod and twice referred to him, but in spite of Hesiod's reputation as a poet of antiquity I can find no evidence that Thoreau read his works.

4. *Writings*, VIII, 496–7; September 12, 1851. See also *ibid.*, IX, 37, 71, 174–5, 235.

5. *Ibid.*, IX, 219–20. In this passage he mentions the Greek poet Menander by name.

6. *Ibid.*, IX, 342. See also *ibid.*, IX, 222: "The telegraph harp reminds me of Anacreon. . . . I could find a name for every strain or intonation of the harp from one or other of the Grecian bards. I often hear Mimnermus, often Menander." This raises the question of just what Thoreau did read in the Greek lyrists outside of Pindar and Anacreon. He quoted Simonides' epigram on Anacreon at the beginning of his Anacreon translations. He once quoted from memory the English translation of one of Sappho's odes, "Sweet mother! I can weave the web no more, So much I love the youth, so much I lingering

The prophecy began to come true in the spring of 1852. One cannot read the journal of that spring without a sense of mounting excitement, partly from the account of the awakening year and partly from the quickening in Thoreau: "I came near awaking this morning, I am older than last year; the mornings are further between; the days are fewer. . . . Oh, might I always wake to thought and poetry—regenerated!"[7] "I go forth to make new demands on life. . . . May I attain to a youth never attained! I am eager to report the glory of the universe; may I be worthy to do it . . ."[8] It was not yet a clear case of recovery. There were many barren times and many almost contradictory reports, inspiration side by side with depression,[9] but by mid-July of 1852 Thoreau could feel that he was attaining his longed-for Indian summer, the period of second growth.

Trees have commonly two growths in the year, a spring and a fall growth, the latter sometimes equalling the former, and you can see where the first was checked whether by cold or drouth, and wonder what there was in the summer to produce this check, this blight. So is it with man; most have a spring growth only, and never get over this first check to their youthful hopes; but plants of hardier constitution, or perchance planted in a more genial soil, speedily recover themselves, and, though they bear the scar or knot in remembrance of their disapointment, they push forward again and have a vigorous fall growth, which is equivalent to a new spring.[1]

That it was Indian summer, second growth, aftermath, Thoreau knew quite well. Occasionally he tried to convince himself that it was preferable to the wild enthusiasm of youth; but for the most part his recovery consisted of a sensible adjustment to altered circumstances. When he relinquished the supernatural, nature was still there; when he ceased to strive for the supersensory, he recovered the satisfactions of the senses. Taste, sight, and sound became again pleasures in his life. It was actually to sound, to the sound of the telegraph harp, that Thoreau seemed to attribute his cure.

I never hear it without thinking of Greece. How the Greeks *harped* upon the words immortal, ambrosial! They are what it says. It stings my ear with everlasting truth. It allies Concord to Athens and both to Elysium. It always intoxicates me, makes me sane, reverses my views of things. . . . This wire

---

love." (W. E. Channing, *Thoreau, the Poet-Naturalist* [Boston, Goodspeed, 1902], p. 184.) This came, however, from a nonclassical anthology of verse. He also quoted part of the Archilochian fragment, "He who fights and runs away, will live to fight another day" (*Writings*, I, 334), but this was so common a quotation that he may not even have known its source. Beyond this rather slight evidence I have found nothing.

7. *Writings*, x, 198. See also *ibid.*, IX, 322–3, 343.

8. *Ibid.*, IX, 351.

9. *Ibid.*, IX, 363, 366; x, 469; XI, 16–17; VI, 193; letter to Sophia, July 13, 1852; *ibid.*, VI, 194; letter to Blake, July 21, 1852.

1. *Ibid.*, x, 227–8; July 14, 1852.

is my redeemer. It always brings a special and a general message to me from the Highest.[2]

The morning wind forever blows; the poem of the world is uninterrupted, but few are the ears that hear it. Forever, that strain of the harp that soothed the Cerberus and called me back to life is sounding.[3]

It seems ridiculous for a man to talk of being restored to sanity by the sound of the wind in the telegraph wires. But Thoreau's loss of sanity, if such it was, was occasioned by the loss of his ideal world, that world of complete harmony of whose life and movement sphere music was the inaudible manifestation. In Thoreau's mind the Grecian Age was the nearest possible earthly approximation of this ideal world, the most perfect mode of life in the history of man; it was the age of music and poetry, the "silent and melodious age." Just as sphere music had once opened the way into the other world, so the sound of the telegraph harp brought before him now the vision of Greece and the Grecian Age. It was a vision which had furnished him inspiration in youth, example in the Walden years; it is not unreasonable that it could furnish him recovery in disease or that, adjusting himself to substitutes, Thoreau could find the telegraph harp and Greece a tolerable compensation for sphere music and the ideal world.

Again it seems melodramatic for Thoreau to speak in terms of sanity. But there were many such expressions, the strongest of them inserted without any drama at all in parentheses in the middle of a description of a brook!

I hear the sound of the piano below as I write this, and feel as if the winter in me were at length beginning to thaw, for my spring has been even more backward than nature's. For a month past life has been a thing incredible. None but the kind gods can make me sane.[4]

The gods did not make him sane; he made himself sane. The gods did not restore to him the things of his youth; he adjusted himself to their loss. Whatever the cause and whatever the cure of his disease, there is no doubt of its seriousness or its nature. Thoreau had been a youthful mystic; in middle age he lost the ability to enter the ecstatic state. Mysticism may be delusion or the only reality; it may be the gift of the gods or it may be mental derangement. But whether it is the bread of life or opium, its withdrawal usually means catastrophe for those who have partaken of it. That Thoreau survived its withdrawal is a sign of his real strength, his "hardier constitution."

It would have been easier had he been able to persuade himself that his earlier experiences were delusion, but he always believed them real,

2. *Ibid.,* x, 458–9; January 9, 1853.
3. *Ibid.,* XI, 200; May 30, 1853. The reference is to the story of Orpheus and Eurydice.
4. *Ibid.,* IX, 398; April 11, 1852.

nor did he then or later deny the principles on which he had built his life. He believed that the defect was in himself:

I have not yet learned to live . . . and I fear that I shall not very soon. I find, however, that in the long run things correspond to my original idea . . . The day is never so dark, nor the night even, but that the laws at least of light prevail, and so may make it light in our minds if they are open to the truth. There is considerable danger that a man will be crazy between dinner and supper; but it will not directly answer any good purpose that I know of, and it is just as easy to be sane.[5]

The last sentence is good Yankee horse sense. Thoreau had no mind to be crazy between noon and night; when he knew that the aspirations of his youth were not going to be realized, he gave up "vain expectations" and settled down to carry out faithfully the many little purposes in life.[6]

As the disease had made little outward show, so the recovery involved little outward change. The journal went on much as before, steadily more particular and circumstantial; there would have been no point in reverting to the old attempt at universal perspective. There was more biographical fact and less personal comment. But whenever the personal comment appeared, it reflected Thoreau's knowledge that his life was a diminishment of its former self. He acknowledged that fact on the day when he first felt confident of his eventual restoration to mental health, and he expressed it consistently thereafter in the themes of lost youth and failing senses.[7] But he expressed at the same time a cheerful acceptance of his limitations.[8]

The changed character of his life showed itself in the continuation and strengthening of the trends of thought which began during the years of disillusionment. His interest in myth had been steadily shifting from past to present. Now he completed the change of direction. It was no longer that the moderns were like the ancients but that the ancients were like the moderns. He idealized the present and the local. In America,

5. *Ibid.*, VI, 242; letter to Blake, December 19, 1854. See also an earlier letter to Blake, *ibid.*, VI, 210-11, and a later one, VI, 316, expressing his belief in his original principles.
6. *Ibid.*, XV, 37.
7. *Ibid.*, X, 227; July 14, 1852: "The youth gets together his materials to build a bridge to the moon, or perchance a temple on earth, and at length the middle-aged man concludes to build a woodshed with them." See also *ibid.*, X, 460: "How much—how, perhaps, all—that is best in our experience in middle life may be resolved into the memory of our youth! I remember how I expanded. If the genius visits me now I am not quite taken off my feet, but I remember how this experience is like, but less than, that I had long since." See also *ibid.*, XII, 53, 80, 165, 225, 363; XIII, 491; XIV, 269; XV, 243; XVII, 89; XIX, 35, 69-70.
8. *Ibid.*, VI, 294; letter to Blake, December 6, 1856: "It is surprising how contented one can be with nothing definite,—only a sense of existence." For earlier and later expressions of the same idea see *ibid.*, XI, 16-17; XII, 190-1, 426; XIV, 294; XV, 37, 160, 244-5; XVI, 133, 202; XVII, 130.

in New England, in Concord was his heaven.[9] Here in a new land, not built on the ruins of antiquity, all that was fairest and most poetic in antiquity was realized. If Leonidas was brave against the enemy at Thermopylae, little Johnny Riordan in his ragged coat daily waged a braver battle against the cold. Bill Wheeler reduced life to a greater simplicity than did Diogenes. John Brown was more a hero than Cato. Every fact and every natural phenomenon was myth; Thoreau would write it.[1] Mythology had served Thoreau first as a field for research, then for critical interpretation; now he had reached the creative stage.

His interest in the antislavery movement was a natural result of that questioning of the authority of government which he had begun in "Civil Disobedience." It was also one more example of his acceptance of substitutes; shut out from the world of ideal beauty and order which he liked to call *kosmos,* he turned his attention to the creation of a better world about him. July, 1854, saw the delivery of his lecture "Slavery in Massachusetts," to be followed later by the John Brown writings.

It was in 1854 that he took up again serious reading in the classics. Going to Fair Haven by boat he tried to recall Homer's description of the waves and could not find the right words, for he had done no reading in Greek since 1849 and the language had grown unfamiliar to him.[2] He apparently repaired the lapse, for he used the proper expression the next year in "Cape Cod."[3] But even then, when he wanted to read the *Antigone* for the third time, he did not venture to try the Greek alone; he borrowed from the Harvard library an edition which contained an English translation.[4]

Most of his classical reading at this time was done in the husbandry writers, of whom he had made a preliminary investigation in 1851. He now renounced purely literary reading: "If the writers of the brazen age are most suggestive to thee, confine thyself to them, and leave those of the Augustan age to dust and the bookworms."[5] Except for a brief and unsatisfactory excursion into Lucretius, Thoreau did confine himself almost exclusively for the next few years to Cato, Varro, Columella, and Palladius.[6] In 1854 he apparently finished Cato and began to read

9. *Ibid.,* IX, 95: "And this is my home, my native soil; and I am a New-Englander. . . . Here have I my habitat. I am of thee." See also *ibid.,* X, 263; XIII, 104–5; XIV, 204; XV, 104, 160; XVI, 118; XVII, 274–5; XVIII, 175, 233, 397.

1. For these statements and others on the same theme see *ibid.,* IX, 99, 149–50, 196; X, 276; XI, 135; IV, 441; V, 233.

2. *Ibid.,* XII, 247.

3. See App. B, "Homer," for quotations from Homer in "Cape Cod."

4. See App. A, No. 48.

5. *Writings,* XII, 68; January 14, 1854.

6. He read the first two hundred lines of Lucretius (*ibid.,* XIV, 312; April 26, 1856) and was impressed by only two (Lucretius, *De rerum natura* i, 72–3, lines in admiration of Prometheus). He must have found Lucretius a metaphysician rather than a poet or a naturalist. Thoreau continued during this period to quote from Vergil and Homer. The quotation from Vergil (*Ecloques* 8 and *Georgics* 1) did not necessarily indicate new read-

Varro and Columella.[7] In 1856 he borrowed an English edition of Columella from the Harvard library and used the Latin and English editions concurrently.[8] In May of the same year he was reading Palladius.[9] It seems likely that he did not finish Palladius for there is little of him in the journals. The last trace of reading in the *Rei rusticae* appeared in the published journal for October 25, 1857.[1]

There seems little pattern to Thoreau's literary-agricultural interests except that which normally determines any interest in any reading—general familiarity and occasional novelty. Thoreau copied directions for buying farms, planting crops, conserving soil, caring for oxen, selecting workmen and watchdogs, making bread and cakes, planting vineyards and nurseries, cramming geese, fattening swine, keeping bees, preparing remedies and charms for sick livestock.

In Cato several ideas won his specific approbation. He approved Cato's emphatically expressed admiration for the rustic life. Watching the careless destruction of forests around Concord, he wished that the superstitions of Cato's time on the sacredness of groves were still in force.[2] Reading Cato's instructions for the use of dry leaves, he regretted that modern farmers did not make better use of them; he wondered whether there might not be a good lecture written on leaves.[3] He was always looking for the worthy subject for the great book.

He did write under Cato's influence a delightful little essay on "How to Catch a Pig."[4] It copies the quaint matter-of-factness of all Cato's instructional writing and is so thoroughly Catonian that it might momentarily deceive the reader were it not for its author's recently journalized experience in pig catching and for the flippancy of the conclusion.

---

ing. Thoreau might even have found his Vergil at this time in a secondary source, for there were many quotations from Vergil in the husbandry writers. Thoreau's quotations from Homer were specific enough to suggest current reading. See App. B for quotations from Vergil and Homer.

7. For Thoreau's quotation from these authors see App. B.

8. See App. A, No. 49.   9. *Writings*, XIV, 329.

1. *Ibid.*, XVI, 126. The editors of the journal have omitted in the published version certain material from the husbandry writers which appears in the *Manuscript Journals* (*MA. 1302*) : from Cato and Varro (*Manuscript Journals*, August 19, 1853–February 12, 1854; *Writings*, XII, January 19, 1854) ; from Columella (*Manuscript Journals*, May 13, 1855–January 3, 1856; *Writings*, XIV, December 30, 1855; *Manuscript Journals*, January 4–April 23, 1856; *Writings*, XIV, April 20, 22, 1856; *Manuscript Journals*, April 23–September 6, 1856; *Writings*, XIV, April 23, 26, 1856, May 7, 1856) ; from Palladius (*Manuscript Journals*, April 23–September 6, 1856; *Writings*, XIV, May 10, 11, 1856, August, 1856). The omitted selections from Cato and Varro come from Bk. i; from Columella, from Bks. i, ii, viii, ix, x; from Palladius, from Bks. i and viii. There are perhaps fifty manuscript pages of this material, a mélange of quotation, summary, and comment, liberally larded with Latin husbandry terms and with cross references from one author to another. They offer proof of the extent of Thoreau's reading in the husbandry writers; they contribute no essential information.

2. *Writings*, XII, 72–3. See also *ibid.*, II, 276–7.

3. *Ibid.*, IX, 61, 63; XV, 191.   4. *Ibid.*, XV, 260.

Varro, like Cato, was emphatic in praise of the farmer's life. And there were certain other things in Varro which attracted Thoreau's attention. The music of the swineherd's horn seemed to him a poetic idea. He liked the classification of man's occupations by times of the day and seasons of the year. He was deeply interested in Varro's philology, and commented frequently on his derivations of words. Sometimes amused by Varro's imagination,[5] Thoreau must have enjoyed in his philology the same thing that he did in Ovid's mythology, the how-things-came-to-be quality.

Selections from Columella were fewer in number but similar in content to those from Varro, except for the absence of philological information and for extra attention to religious rites and customs. Columella also opened up new reading possibilities by giving a list of fifty authors who had written before him on the same subjects; Thoreau never failed to utilize such a list.[6] From Palladius he took almost nothing; he noticed the statements of both Columella and Palladius that a swamp was not a healthful building site, and concluded characteristically that when such a statement was true man was not yet at home in nature.[7]

These small specifications are unimportant except as they illustrate once more Thoreau's fidelity to his original ideas. Unimportant too is the opportunity that the husbandry writers gave him to apply his ancient-modern comparisons to prove for the hundredth time that nature and human nature do not change. Of much greater importance certainly is the part they played in providing the solidity and stability which he needed to restore him to mental health. But the thing Thoreau found in the husbandry writers which fitted into both his past and current thinking and which was to shape appreciably the future course of his thought was their emphasis on man's existence as closely bound to the turning of the year, their representation of man leading a seasonal life in nature.

Thoreau had been coming to this view of life through his own experience. He felt the close relationship between his moods and nature. He was extremely susceptible simply to weather, to cloudiness and sunshine, rain and drought. As a result he was generally susceptible to the seasons, regenerated by spring, dazzled and torpid under summer heat, revived by fall, alternately stilled and frozen by winter. Man's correspondence to nature seemed sometimes momentary, sometimes seasonal; sometimes it became an analogy between the seasons of the year and the whole life of man. In this analogy human life became identified with plant or vegetable life, not only as a matter of seasonal growth but as a matter of structure and quality. "There is, no doubt," Thoreau once

5. *Ibid.,* xvi, 126.
6. *Ibid.,* xii, 125. Thoreau found here the names of Aristotle and Theophrastus. He found them also, of course, in English works on natural history.
7. *Ibid.,* xiv, 329–30.

said, "a perfect analogy between the life of the human being and that of the vegetable, both of the body and the mind," and following Gray's botanical disquisition on vegetable life he worked out a four-page analogy.[8] Eventually he made an identification of all forms of life: animal, vegetable, mineral, and spiritual;[9] he seemed to believe in the transmigration of souls;[1] he came at last to assert the identity of all forms either of life or of matter, things animate or inanimate.[2] There were all levels of existence and degrees of life. He thought that the tortoise was probably the lowest form of animal life, nearest to the vegetable.[3] Planting tortoise eggs in the earth, watching their development, waiting for them to hatch, he pondered on the life that goes on under the surface of the earth, eventually to emerge. He saw the globe as organic, layer upon layer of unfolding life: "How much lies quietly buried in the ground that we wot not of!"[4] "There is nothing inorganic. This earth is not, then, a mere fragment of dead history, strata upon strata, like the leaves of a book . . . but living poetry, like the leaves of a tree,—not a fossil earth, but a living specimen."[5]

It was this idea that brought him back again to the search for the pattern of the forms. In the earth itself, in the foliate patterns of the sand in the Cut, he found "an anticipation of the vegetable leaf," in the "vital" earth evidence of the law of unity.[6]

These theories, that man was a part of a living nature, closely linked to every form of life and matter, and that his life showed a perfect correspondence to nature, merged into an overwhelming literary theory. If he could chart the pattern of a year he would have the pattern of life. For as the leaf obsessed him as a material pattern, so the year fascinated him as a pattern of the operation of nature. He saw the same circle repeated in time; he saw it repeated analogically in miniature in the pattern of the day[7] and expanded into the life span of man. If he could capture and put down all the phenomena of the year he would have

---

8. *Ibid.,* VIII, 201–5.

9. *Ibid.,* IX, 219; X, 410; XII, 483; XVIII, 23, 113; XIX, 242–3.

1. *Ibid.,* VIII, 271: "It is unavoidable, the idea of transmigration; not merely a fancy of the poets, but an instinct of the race."

2. *Ibid.,* XII, 278: "Who shall distinguish between the *law* by which a brook finds its river, the *instinct* [by which] a bird performs its migrations, and the *knowledge* by which a man steers his ship round the globe?" See also *ibid.,* XII, 62.

3. *Ibid.,* XII, 276, 474.

4. *Ibid.,* XII, 474. See also for the same idea in the same context *ibid.,* XIII, 28.

5. *Ibid.,* XII, 99–100. See also *ibid.,* VIII, 169; IX, 165.

6. *Ibid.,* XII, 148: "On the outside all the life of the earth is expressed in the animal or vegetable, but make a deep cut in it and you find it vital; you find in the very sands an anticipation of the vegetable leaf. . . . No wonder that the earth expresses itself outwardly in leaves, which labors with the idea thus inwardly. The overhanging leaf sees here its prototype. The earth is pregnant with law." All of Thoreau's writing on the sand foliage centered in this idea.

7. *Ibid.,* XI, 393.

the secret. Or he could come at it another way. The biography of the poet, the record of his moods and thoughts, should be the same thing, for the seasons and phenomena of the year were phenomena and phases of the life of man.[8] The pattern of the year and the pattern of a man's thoughts should be identical, should make the same great poem.

He was tempted to try a chart of the year. Here was use for all the accumulation of fact that he had stored up and was continuing to store up in the journal. Then he wanted to graph man's correspondence to the chart.

Why should just these sights and sounds accompany our life? Why should I hear the chattering of blackbirds, why smell the skunk each year? I would fain explore the mysterious relation between myself and these things. I would at least know what these things unavoidably are, make a chart of our life, know how its shores trend, that butterflies reappear and when, know why just this circle of creatures completes the world.[9]

The first step was the chart of fact, marking down that butterflies and birds and flowers and snowstorms and certain temperatures and even forest trees reappear and when. He made a chart once of the phenomena of March. But he early complained that nature was so vast that man could never see even one of her features; he felt he came too late into the world to find the record complete.[1] He could not manage the whole book, and he tried to divide it into parts: a chapter on snowdrifts, an epic on winter, the poem of spring, a lecture on leaves, a book of buds, a book of autumn tints. The last he partially realized.[2]

If charting the year was too big a task, charting man's correspondence to it was more colossal yet; he did not make a very serious attempt to do it. Had he tried, it would have constituted another attempt to discover the answer and another failure, and Thoreau was convinced now of the inscrutability of nature. Not by prying would man find the secret. He was almost superstitious about the matter. He must not walk with direction but with a kind of sauntering carelessness. He must not observe with intent but casually, see with the "side of the eye," hear with

8. *Ibid.*, VIII, 403; XVI, 127: "These regular phenomena of the seasons get at last to be— they were *at first*, of course, simply and plainly phenomena or phases of my life. The seasons and all their changes are in me. . . . The perfect correspondence of Nature to man, so that he is at home in her!" *Ibid.*, XV, 407: "A year is made up of a certain series and number of sensations and thoughts which have their language in nature. . . . Each experience reduces itself to a mood of the mind." *Ibid.*, XVIII, 159: "The moods and thoughts of man are revolving just as steadily and incessantly as nature's." See also *ibid.*, XI, 393–5; XVIII, 347.

9. *Ibid.*, IX, 438.

1. *Ibid.*, VIII, 77; V, 242; XIV, 221: "I am reminded that this my life in nature, this particular round of natural phenomena which I call a year, is lamentably incomplete. I listen to a concert in which so many parts are wanting."

2. *Ibid.*, IX, 186–7; XV, 168, 270, 191; XVI, 258; XI, 516; XVII, 254.

the "side of the ear."[3] He knew also his own limitations of age and illness. To combat them he maintained a discipline of his body designed to keep it as sensitive as possible to every stimulus. He urged himself to early rising, to avoidance of tea and coffee, to temperance in all things including society. He would be temperate even in eating fruit and drinking water.[4] Watching himself closely, being careful not to watch nature too closely, he might stumble upon a scrap of truth now and then.

He could not keep from speculating on the correspondences. Why should just certain things appear in a man's life in nature? What were a meadow and an island in his experience? What did these hieroglyphics of hills and rivers mean? What was the relationship between the bird that sang and the ear that heard? Certainly one was made for the other? What was the rainbow? Surely it was not to be explained scientifically. Might it be God's face?[5] For as he asked he kept trying to answer. The answers were fragmentary: a waterfall was the rush of the blood in his veins; a flower expressed a mood of the mind; the owls were his own "stark, unsatisfied thoughts"; sparrows too were thoughts he had; the snow was like waves, like steam; the earth star and the snow star were identical; crystals, leaves, fishes, too, were all symbolic; nature herself a huge symbol of man's thought.[6]

Years ago, speaking of myth and the futility of trying to find a literal significance for it, he had said, "It is like striving to make the sun, or the wind, or the sea symbols to signify exclusively the particular thoughts of our day. But what signifies it?"[7] He may very well have been asking himself the same question now. He wrote to a friend who had asked his opinion of Swedenborg:

He comes nearer to answering, or attempting to answer, literally, your questions concerning man's origin, purpose, and destiny, than any of the worthies I have referred to. But I think that is not *altogether* a recommendation; since such an answer to these questions cannot be discovered any more than perpetual motion, for which no reward is now offered.[8]

"But what signifies it?" He did not expect an answer. He still thought in terms of the actual and the ideal, but he no longer thought of the one in any real sense as a symbol of the other. He had lost the sense of connection between the two. He used nature, the actual, as a stimulant;

3. *Ibid.*, xix, 170; viii, 416; xiv, 314, 319; xvi, 164.
4. *Ibid.*, x, 198; xi, 424, 456; xii, 436.
5. *Ibid.*, viii, 107, 160–1; x, 312; xv, 274–5; x, 128; xviii, 44–5. See also *ibid.*, xvi, 134; x, 366.
6. *Ibid.*, viii, 300; xi, 184; ix, 122–3; xvi, 128; viii, 129; xiv, 88; ix, 437; xi, 135. See also *ibid.*, xi, 21.
7. *Ibid.*, i, 61; with slight variation, vii, 392.
8. *Ibid.*, vi, 300; letter to B. B. Wiley, December 12, 1856.

he supplied the ideal from his own imagination. He had always defended the poetical, analogical method against the scientific, but he had tried to make his analogies sound ones, based on fact. Now they came out of his fancy. "We soon get through with nature," he said. "She excites an expectation which she cannot satisfy."[9] The thing itself was not important, only its effect on the beholder.[1] Nor was it the ideal that interested him so much as his own ideal.[2] His questions were merely rhetorical, expressions of wonder that the world should be so full of law and harmony.

Thoreau's next reading in the classics reflected this new view of nature, although it came as a natural extension of an old interest. For years he had been reading English treatises on natural history. It was a way of accumulating data for his chart of the phenomena of nature, an extension of and a check on his own observation. The authors whom he read made frequent mention of the Greek and Roman naturalists and borrowed heavily from them. The Roman husbandry writers too had referred to them. It was inevitable that Thoreau should eventually become curious enough about Pliny and Aristotle and Theophrastus to want to read them. Pliny and Aristotle he must have known fairly well by reputation; Theophrastus he looked up in Lemprière as a preliminary to reading him.[3]

The early naturalists, indeed, provided Thoreau with exactly what he wanted: the sense of worship and wonder which was more important than accurate information,[4] the original and unprejudiced view of nature that belongs to antiquity,[5] and, more specifically, much of the kind of information which really constitutes nature-myth, all combined with a charming disregard for the limitations of fact:

The old naturalists were so sensitive and sympathetic to nature that they could be surprised by the ordinary events of life. It was an incessant miracle to them, and therefore gorgons and fiery dragons were not incredible to them. The greatest and saddest defect is not credulity, but our habitual forgetfulness that our science is ignorance.[6]

"So far as natural history is concerned," he said, "you often have to choose between uninteresting truth and interesting falsehood."[7] Thoreau liked his information interesting.

He began the reading of the naturalists with Pliny, securing for himself a good three-volume Latin edition in the fall of 1859.[8] The same fall

9. *Ibid.*, XII, 293.   1. *Ibid.*, XVI, 165.
2. *Ibid.*, XVII, 282: ". . . our ideal is the only real."
3. *Harvard Fact-Book*, p. 17.   4. *Writings*, XIX, 133.
5. *Ibid.*, XIX, 169.   6. *Ibid.*, XIX, 180.
7. *Ibid.*, XIX, 181. See also *ibid.*, XIX, 160; VIII, 160.
8. See Supplement to App. A, No. 14.

he acquired the English translation of Pliny in the Bohn edition.[9] In December he withdrew from the Harvard library editions of Aristotle and Theophrastus, the first in Greek and French, the second in Greek and Latin.[1] Few signs of his reading in these authors appeared in the journals,[2] but there were great blocks of material from them in *A Book of Extracts*.

Again, as in the case of the husbandry writers, it is difficult to see any definite pattern to Thoreau's reading. As he had been interested in nearly every phase of a Roman farmer's life, so he seemed to be interested in almost every fact in natural history. He compared the information given by the classical writers with that in the later naturalists whom he had read, and he compared the observations of Pliny and Theophrastus and Aristotle with his own. He evinced interest in the familiar frogs and fish and in the unfamiliar elephants and panthers. And he loved the beautiful incredibilities, the honey which fell from the air when there was a rainbow, the Hercynian forests, old as time, where the great roots literally heaved up the earth.

In each of the naturalists he found information or comment that fitted into his own patterns of thought. The first group of selections from Pliny dealt with trees,[3] and Pliny, like Thoreau, had felt the similarity between plant and human life. He spoke of the physical structure of trees, their flesh, bones, fat, veins, fibers. He sketched too the orderly progress of the seasons of the year, the seasons of fecundation, of blossoming, of fruit bearing. He reported that there were trees which bore no fruit and those that never blossomed. "So, too, in life," he moralized, "the fortunes of many men are ever without their time of blossoming."[4] Reminiscent of Thoreau's discussions of the telegraph harp was Pliny's explanation of sound traveling along the grain of wood.

The second group of selections from Pliny dealt with animal life.[5] The subjects ranged from elephants to mice, from panthers to pigs, from dolphins to hares. Under fish were discussed crabs, sea nettles, the nautilus, the oyster, and pearls. The section on insects began with bees and honey and went on to spiders, glowworms, and locusts.

9. See App. A, No. 54. On a separate sheet of paper in the back of the *Manuscript Journals* (*MA. 1302*), April 18–September 21, 1859, he recorded his intention of procuring this book. On December 8, 1859, he quoted from and referred to the Bohn edition in the journal (*Writings*, xix, 17, n. 1).

1. See App. A, Nos. 50–1.

2. For references in the *Writings* see App. C. References to Pliny which are primary rather than secondary are *Writings*, xix, 16–17, 104, 133, and xx, 310, 331, n. 1. Bona fide references to Aristotle are *ibid.*, xix, 55, 77–8; to Theophrastus, *ibid.*, xix, 133, 240.

3. *A Book of Extracts*, pp. 128–37; the selections are from the third volume of Bohn and from Bks. xvi and xvii of Pliny on cultivated and forest trees.

4. Bohn, iii, 380–1; Pliny xvi, 40.

5. *A Book of Extracts*, pp. 146–60; the selections are from Bks. viii, ix, x, and xi of Pliny, dealing with terrestrial animals, fish, birds, and insects.

The third group contained only three selections, Orphic in character.[6] One described the deity as "eternal, without bounds, neither created, nor subject at any time, to destruction." The second defined *kosmos* as beauty in accordance with Thoreau's own idea of the meaning of the word. The third was an Orphic description of the sun.

Thoreau's selections from Theophrastus[7] were inserted between two big sections of material from Pliny, as though he had started to read Theophrastus, tired of him, and gone back to Pliny. That is a reasonable surmise, for Thoreau commented that Theophrastus was too systematic to be interesting and that Pliny had borrowed much from him.[8] The selections all came from the *Historia plantarum*, the *De causis plantarum*, and from the fragments *De coloribus*, *De igne*, and *De signis pluviarum*.[9] Of special interest were the entries from *De coloribus* on the dark color of roughened water, recalling Homer's sea, and those from *De signis pluviarum* on the signs of the weather.[1] As Thoreau became more and more susceptible simply to weather he developed an interest in weather signs. He commented that many later writers had borrowed their information on this subject from Theophrastus without giving credit to the source.

Aristotle Thoreau seemed to regard as too scientific,[2] but he copied more from him than from either of the others, possibly because he did not own an edition of Aristotle and had to write out any information which he might want to find again. He worked through the first volume of the Camus edition of *Histoire des animaux*,[3] which comprised the text, and supplemented it with material from the second volume, containing the author's notes. He continually referred to other writers on the same subjects and annotated his quotation liberally with comment and cross reference.

Thoreau had liked Pliny's attitude of wonder; he must have enjoyed Aristotle's very original point of view, for Aristotle wrote of the animal world as though he were seeing it for the first time as he wrote. He was curiously concerned with the similarity of man to other animals, reporting such fascinating bits of information as that man was the only two-legged creature with feet who had fleshy legs, and remarking certain dissimilarities of structure between men and birds. He thought also that men were the only animals who dreamed, and he drew rather naïve conclusions about the bodily seats of certain mental faculties.

6. *A Book of Extracts*, p. 282; Bohn, I, 15, 17, 20; Pliny ii, 1, 3, 4.
7. *A Book of Extracts*, pp. 138–45.
8. *Ibid.*, p. 138.
9. All of these are from the second volume of the Bohn edition. Thoreau seems to have sampled systematically through the whole volume.
1. For journal reference see *Writings*, xix, 133, 240.
2. *Ibid.*, xviii, 372.
3. For this edition see App. A. No. 51.

If the period at which a man writes is early enough in recorded history he may well be naturalist, historian, and geographer all at once. All of these terms would apply to all three of these naturalists, and they would apply even more aptly to the last group of classical authors that Thoreau read, to Aelian, Herodotus, and Strabo.

Aelian is classified both as naturalist from his *De natura animalium* and as historian from his *Variae historiae*. Although Thoreau withdrew both books from the Harvard library in the spring of 1860, it was from the *Variae historiae* that he took passages for his commonplace book.[4] The *Variae historiae* is a collection of historical and fabulous anecdotes, the kind of history which Thoreau greatly relished, but he seems not to have cared for Aelian; he copied only five anecdotes.[5]

Herodotus came to Thoreau recommended in many areas of knowledge. In the *Harvard Fact-Book* Thoreau has preserved a three-page summary of De Quincey's analysis of Herodotus as a man "nearly related to all literature whatsoever . . . the father of what may be called ethnographical geography . . . a man who speculated most ably on all the *humanities* of science." De Quincey went on to say, "He is a naturalist, the earliest that existed. He is a mythologist, and a speculator on the origin, as well as value, of religious rites. He is a political economist by instinct of genius, before the science of economy had a name or a conscious function . . ." He added that while it was common opinion that Pliny contained the greatest store of ancient learning, he himself maintained that Herodotus provided "by much the largest basis for vast commentaries revealing the archeologies of the human race; whilst, as the eldest of prose writers, he justifies his majestic state as a brotherly assessor on the same throne with Homer."[6]

So Thoreau came finally in the last year of his life to a man who represented in himself nearly all his own interests, a prose Homer. Writing to a friend the damaging confession that he had been reading the New York *Tribune,* he tried to atone for it: "I am reading Herodotus and Strabo . . . as hard as I can, to counterbalance it."[7] It is unfortunate that Thoreau had so little time left for reading and that he left so scanty a record of what he did read. He could easily have read in both Herodotus and Strabo almost identical material: that geography which forms the history of the organic globe, that history which is the history of the human race, and that natural history and nature-myth which tie the two

4. For these books see App. A, Nos. 52, 53.

5. *A Book of Extracts,* pp. 186–7; Aelian i, 3, Egyptian Frogs; i, 33, Mises and the Pomegranate; ii, 28, Cock Fighting; ii, 33, Images of Rivers; vii, 6, Remark of a Certain Scythian about the Cold.

6. *Harvard Fact-Book,* pp. 180–3; *The Collected Writings of Thomas De Quincey,* ed. David Masson (Edinburgh, Adam and Charles Black, 1889), vi, 96–138, *passim.*

7. *Writings,* vi, 379; letter to Parker Pillsbury, April 10, 1861.

together, in other words, "the archeologies of the human race." Most of the reading in Herodotus was of that type,[8] as was some in Strabo, but the greater part of Thoreau's reading in Strabo was concerned with Homer as the first authority for the archaeologies.[9] Strabo insisted that geography properly considered was closely allied with philosophy and with all knowledge; he named Homer not only first poet, first mythologian, first historian, and first naturalist but first geographer. It is a pleasant thought that Thoreau closed his classical study with reading about, if not in, Homer and that for him Homer was still the poet, transmitter of all knowledge.

The classics had gone a long way with Thoreau and had served him in many ways. In utilitarian fashion they had provided material for translation and models for imitation. In them he had found the source, the corroboration, or the extension of most of his favorite theories: of language, of government, of history and myth, of poetry and music, of the sameness of the universe. As a whole they had been for him originally a reference work which he might consult in his search for truth. From a source of information concerning his ideal world they had become a kind of symbol of that world, an encouraging glimpse and a proof of the existence of a still greater and yet surely attainable world. In Thoreau's youth Homer and Vergil had given him such encouraging glimpses; at Walden it was Homer who offered him a working pattern and a relaxed philosophy of living, who permitted him through the reconstruction of the Homeric life to live in part his ideal life; in the depression of the post-Walden years Thoreau found sanative value in the husbandry writers and a gleam of hope in that vision of the Grecian Era evoked by the telegraph harp. When he knew at last that he would not in this world attain the world of which he had dreamed, the Golden Age of the Greeks became an acceptable substitute, a vista on which his eyes might rest with pleasure. During the last years of his life the naturalists, geographers, and anthropologists contributed to that view and helped him pursue his piecemeal investigation of the universe. He came back at last to Homer but at secondhand and with a scientific rather than a poetic approach.

8. For edition of Herodotus see App. A, No. 55. For selections from Herodotus see *A Book of Extracts*, pp. 256–64; Bohn, pp. 94–577, *passim*.

9. He seems to have read approximately the first three hundred pages of the first volume of the Bohn edition of Strabo (Supplement to App. A, No. 15). See *Writings*, xx, 338, n. 2. This material covers Strabo i–iv.

V

Ultimates

So now I would say something . . . to you, my readers. . . .
the time is short . . .

HOWEVER extensive Thoreau's study of the classics had been it was antedated and overshadowed by his interest in the quest. However well he had kept the journal, he kept it not for itself but for a record of the search, first as an account of progress and later as a collection of data. Some months before he died he ceased both to read in the classics and to write in his journal; he laid aside the tool and closed the account. What then of the quest? Was it left unfinished and the question unanswered?

It was one of Thoreau's strongest convictions that the poet must publish his truth both in words and in his life, and it is then in his last words and last days that we must look for results. We know that he had long ago given up finding the answer that he had in his youth so confidently expected. Did he find anything worth reporting in his twenty-five years' search?

Thoreau spent the last year of his life working with the journals, selecting from their bulk what he wanted to say to the world. He produced five articles: "Autumnal Tints," "Night and Moonlight," "Wild Apples," "Life without Principle," and "Walking."[1] It is singular that nearly all the material for these articles comes from the journal of the early 1850's, the years of his worst discouragement; but the tone is completely changed. He has taken the circumstances and facts which were the cause of his despair and converted them to a solid basis for final satisfaction.

"Autumnal Tints," "Night and Moonlight," and "Wild Apples" are chapters from that half-seriously projected book which should chart the phenomena of nature and the thoughts of man to show the pattern of life but which was too immense in scope ever to be written. "Autumnal Tints" is the least of the three, a fragmentary chart of nature only, but it recalls the journal speculations on the proper subject for the great book and the tentative suggestions for smaller units of writing.[2] "Night

---

1. There is much classical quotation and reference in these articles, but none of it is new.
2. *Writings*, v, 251.

and Moonlight" admirably illustrates Thoreau's technique of turning the unhappy passages of the earlier journal into expressions of optimism. In 1851 he had found his interest in night and moonlight "ominous"; he had shrunk from light; he had spoken with sympathetic attraction of the "cold excitement of lunacy." Now ten years later he writes of the calm beauty of the night as a phase of nature too little appreciated, and he concludes the essay with one of his little analogies between natural phenomena and the feelings of men: "Nevertheless, even by night the sky is blue and not black, for we see through the shadow of the earth into the distant atmosphere of day, where the sunbeams are reveling."[3]

This is personal experience, impersonalized and generalized from a ten years' perspective. The same technique is employed in "Wild Apples." The long description of the thwarted but persistent growth of the wild apple tree concludes, "What a lesson to man! So are human beings, referred to the highest standard, the celestial fruit which they suggest and aspire to bear, browsed on by fate; and only the most persistent and strongest genius defends itself and prevails, sends a tender scion upward at last, and drops its perfect fruit on the ungrateful earth."[4] This is much like Thoreau's 1852 comparison of a man and a tree.[5] What he said then in hope he could say now as fact.

"Life without Principle" is more specifically an attempt to communicate conclusions. Thoreau prefaces it with a statement of intention. Speaking of his desire as a lecturer and a poet to "deal with his privatest experience," he adds, "So now I would say something similar to you, my readers. . . . As the time is short, I will leave out all the flattery, and retain all the criticism."[6] He goes on to demand, "Let us consider the way in which we spend our lives."[7] "Life without Principle" is much like *Walden* in its hortatory quality; it deplores the mode of life of most men and urges them to devote themselves to solider realities than business or money. It admits its author's poverty of communicable truth: "I do not know why my news should be so trivial,—considering what one's dreams and expectations are, why the developments should be so paltry."[8] It insists upon the revelatory aspect of knowledge: "Knowledge does not come to us by details, but in flashes of light from heaven."[9] It contains Thoreau's declaration, already quoted in Chapter 1, that he has been since boyhood and is still engaged in a very serious enterprise.[1] We might reasonably make the same complaint of Thoreau that he made of earlier poets for the vague and slight character of the truth they published; when he tried to say something to his readers he could say only

3. *Ibid.*, v, 333.
5. *Ibid.*, x, 227–8. See above, p. 72.
7. *Ibid.*
9. *Ibid.*, iv, 475–6.

4. *Ibid.*, v, 307.
6. *Ibid.*, iv, 456.
8. *Ibid.*, iv, 471–2.
1. *Ibid.*, iv, 460.

that he was convinced of the value of the principles by which he had lived, however immaterial their results might seem.

While "Life without Principle" is an open letter of advice to the public, "Walking" is Thoreau's personal apologia. In its allegory the outward way in which he spent much of his life becomes the symbol of his inner activity. He begins with a definition of sauntering, which is his definition of living.[2] He lists the requirements for a walker in terms which are biblical in source and religious in meaning: "If you are ready to leave father and mother, and brother and sister, and wife and child and friends, and never see them again,—if you have paid your debts, and made your will, and settled all your affairs, and are a free man, then you are ready for a walk."[3] He points out the path, westward and forward rather than eastward and back: "We go eastward to realize history and study the works of art and literature, retracing the steps of the race; we go westward as into the future, with a spirit of enterprise and adventure."[4] He warns that a man's discoveries will not be communicable fact but inner certainty:

The highest that we can attain to is not Knowledge, but Sympathy with Intelligence. I do not know that this higher knowledge amounts to anything more definite than a novel and grand surprise on a sudden revelation of the insufficiency of all that we called Knowledge before,—a discovery that there are more things in heaven and earth than are dreamed of in our philosophy. It is the lighting up of the mist by the sun. Man cannot *know* in any higher sense than this, any more than he can look serenely and with impunity in the face of the sun . . .[5]

This passage too has its source in a similar statement from Thoreau's years of discouragement;[6] but while the utterance of 1851 expressed a reluctant relinquishment of the definite character of knowledge, now the emphasis is on the grandeur of a knowledge that defies finite comprehension.

The image of the illuminating sun appears again in the closing lines in which Thoreau describes briefly his approach toward death: "So we saunter toward the Holy Land, till one day the sun shall shine more brightly than ever he has done, shall perchance shine into our minds and hearts, and light up our whole lives with a great awakening light, as warm and serene and golden as on a bankside in autumn."[7]

"Walking" has about it the sense of finality; it is a finished presentation of a philosophy of life, complete with an evaluation of the philosophy. On the one hand it denies for itself the achievement of material results and on the other insists on the sure existence and value of an immaterial achievement. That is not unusual. Most religions and philoso-

2. *Ibid.*, v, 205–6.
3. *Ibid.*, v, 206.
4. *Ibid.*, v, 218.
5. *Ibid.*, v, 240.
6. *Ibid.*, viii, 168; 1851.
7. *Ibid.*, v, 247–8.

phies and many nonreligious and nonphilosophical codes of behavior embody some such belief. But Thoreau's belief was unusual in that he offered it not as theory or doctrine but as a fact of which he was certain on the basis of experience. And it was unusual that the experience on which he based his certainty was not simply mystic experience. For over a decade now he had not been able to realize the ecstatic state. Thoreau's certainty was a sober one, a reality that the disappointments and limitations of his last years could not diminish.

That he had attained a genuine certainty not only his last words but the last days of his life attest. He was so sure of the rightness of things that he was quite undisturbed by the knowledge of his approaching death, not courageous or resigned but cheerfully serene and confident. His sister Sophia wrote of him shortly before he died, "Henry . . . is so happy . . ." She urged his friends to come to see him and "be cheered." His behavior was so genuinely convincing that not even the sister or the mother could grieve.[8]

That certainty was the only answer at the end of the quest. Still it is an answer for which most men would probably be willing to trade their trivial lives if they could understand what it means or believe it attainable. It is, however, one of the realities which are purely personal, nontransferable, and not even explicable at second hand. The surprising thing is that so many men in the history of mankind have made such discoveries and have attempted to communicate them to others. But the communication is always unsuccessful. When such men are far enough back in time we call them prophets or seers or saints and thus remove them to a category where we need not deal with them factually. If they are too close to us and too open in their confidences we call them mad. We have had a hard time doing either to Thoreau; he was obviously neither saint nor madman. We have had no recourse but to call him an enigma, which is another way of saying that we do not understand him. Yet no one ever made a clearer statement of intentions or pursued them more openly. He began with an hypothesis which to most men seems impossible and ended with a proof which to most men seems incomprehensible, but between the two extremes his life appears consistent and logical.

8. Sanborn, *The First and Last Journeys of Thoreau*, II, 127.

APPENDIX A

Classical Books Used by Thoreau

Prefatory Note

IN COMPILING the list of classical books which Thoreau either owned or read, I have included with the texts and translations of Greek and Latin authors other books which serve the purpose of classical study: Greek and Latin dictionaries, grammars, collections of quotations and antiquities, and studies of the character and customs of the Greeks and Romans. I have omitted works which, although in a sense classical, belong primarily to some other field: ancient histories, histories of philosophy, and such books as the Latin Linnaeus and the Latin Gray, which have no claim for consideration except the language in which they are written.

I have listed the books, as far as possible, in the order of Thoreau's use or acquisition. Except when otherwise noted, I have taken the bibliographical data from the title pages of the books, preserving the original capitalization, spelling, and punctuation, but eliminating without special notation much nonessential descriptive material. In cases where I could not determine the exact edition of a work, I have indicated uncertainty either by a question mark after the date of publication or by specific comment on the subject. Each bibliographical description is followed by the source or sources from which the identification was established and by any information of special interest concerning the book or Thoreau's use of it. I have used symbols to designate sources repeated frequently.

The Harvard College catalogues proved a valuable source of information. The entrance requirements given in the catalogues for 1830–33 helped to identify academy texts. The courses of instruction and the annual presidential reports in the catalogues from 1833–36 gave information about Harvard texts. This information was supplemented by the advertisements of the university booksellers and publishers inserted in the catalogue and by *A Select Catalog of Books Chiefly Published or Imported,* published in 1837 by Hilliard, Gray, and Company of Boston, who were, under some variety of name, booksellers to the university.[1] The Harvard entrance requirements have been designated by the symbol HER; the courses of instruction, HCI; the presidential reports, HPR; the booksellers' advertisements in the college catalogues, HBA; and the publishers' catalogue, PC, followed by the page number.

The best single source of information is Thoreau's own library list in the *Index Rerum (HM945)* in Huntington Library; it has been printed by

1. The name of the firm changed often, using various combinations of the names Brown, Hilliard, Little, Gray, Wilkins, and others. I have used the earliest catalogue available in the Yale library; Little, Brown and Company, modern successors to the firm, have none earlier.

Sanborn with his usual inaccuracies in his book, *Henry David Thoreau,* pp. 505–17. The list is in three sections: books acquired by 1836, books acquired 1836–40, and books acquired after 1840. The divisions of the list are not always clear, and the bibliographical data varies from reasonable completeness to such vague notation as "Orpheus 1 v." I have referred to the three sections of this list as A, B, and C.

Sanborn has also printed in *Henry David Thoreau,* pp. 520–1 a reading list labeled "A List of Authors Read or to be Read by H. D. Thoreau." This is little more than an ambitious outline of classical literature; inclusion of a work on this list is in no way evidence that Thoreau read it. The list can be considered only when the specification is so detailed as to indicate that Thoreau either had done the reading or had planned it carefully enough to show a definite intention.

Other lists have been helpful: Thoreau's brief reading list in *HM13201,* the Fruitlands library list,[2] the Wakeman Collection catalogue,[3] and Cameron's list of Thoreau's borrowings from the Harvard library.[4] Thoreau has identified some few books either in his journals or his commonplace books. When all other means of identification have failed I have had recourse to the laborious method of checking Thoreau's text and page references with all available editions of the work in question.

There are two clues to information which I have been unable to pursue successfully; I give them for the possible benefit of others. On June 22, 1856, Daniel Ricketson wrote in his diary, "Spent the forenoon in H.D.T.'s room, copying titles of books, &c."[5] If this list could be found, it might lead to the identification of some books. The clue to the other source comes from two book lists which have at some time been laid in the *Index Rerum,* but which do not belong to the manuscript itself: one, a list of Thoreau's books owned by F. H. Bigelow in 1872; the other, a list of Thoreau's books once owned by Elizabeth Weir. Since Mr. Bigelow and Miss Weir seem to have possessed most of the difficult-to-identify books, the discovery of the disposition of their libraries might solve a number of puzzles.

When I have had reason to believe that Thoreau may have read some classical work, but have not been able to make any adequate identification, I have listed the book in the Supplement to Appendix A, giving whatever information is available concerning it.

1. P. Virgilii Maronis Opera. ad usum Serenissimi Delphini. Juxta Editionem novissimam Londiniensem. Philadelphia: Printed by A. Small, for M. Carey & Son 1817.

2. This is printed in C. E. Sears, *Bronson Alcott's Fruitlands* (Boston and New York, Houghton Mifflin, 1915), pp. 177–85, and in the *Dial,* III, No. 4 (April, 1843), 545–8.

3. The *Stephen H. Wakeman Collection of Books of American Writers* (New York, American Art Association, Inc., 1924).

4. A check of all libraries to which Thoreau could have had access revealed no classical borrowings from any other library.

5. Anna Ricketson, *Daniel Ricketson and His Friends* (Boston and New York, Houghton Mifflin, 1902), p. 288.

HER; *HM945*, A & B: Thoreau had two copies of this book. One (Wakeman Collection, Item 1056) was given by Sophia to Elizabeth Weir. It is autographed "D. H. Thoreau. Hollis 20, Sept 4th." It contains the entire Latin text of Vergil supplemented by a marginal prose "interpretation" which is equivalent to a translation and must have obviated any student difficulty with poetic diction.

2. M. T. Ciceronis Orationes quaedam selectae, Bostoniae: Hilliard, Gray, Little, et Wilkins 1831.

HER; *HM945*, A: Thoreau's copy is now in the possession of Abernethy Library at Middlebury College. The flyleaf bears the autograph "H. D. Thoreau." This is a European text, edited by Charles Folsom. It contains the four orations against Catiline, the second Philippic, and the orations for the Manilian law, for Marcellus, Ligerius, King Deiotarus, the poet Archias, and Milo. This is more material than a high school student would read now, but Thoreau's study of it may have been selective rather than comprehensive.

3. The Greek Reader, by Frederic Jacobs, Boston: Hilliard, Gray, Little, and Wilkins. 1829 (?).

HER; PC, p. 93: This is a condensation of a four-volume *Elementarbuch* by a contemporary German scholar, edited by Edward Everett of Harvard and revised by John Pickering, eminent American classicist. It has Pickering's specialty, the Greek-English rather than the Greek-Latin lexicon; it contains an assortment of rather anecdotal prose selections of wide variety: natural history, mythology, geography, history, biography, and philosophy; there are a few pages from the *Iliad*.

4. Stereotype Edition. Adam's Latin Grammar, By Benjamin A. Gould, Master of the Public Latin-School of Boston. Boston: Hilliard, Gray, Little, and Wilkins; and Richardson and Lord. 1829.

HER; *HM945*, A: This book was adopted by Harvard and specifically recommended to those preparing to enter. Thoreau referred to it in a letter to Helen (*Writings*, VI, 25; October 6, 1838), suggesting that she consult it on Latin pronunciation; his description of the book identifies it as this one, not as No. 5 below, another Adam's grammar. Benjamin Gould was one of many editors of the grammar of Alexander Adam of Edinburgh. Edward Everett Hale in his *New England Boyhood* (Boston, Little, Brown, 1927), pp. 27–8, refers to this grammar as "very bad" and gives an interesting account of the method by which it was taught.

5. The Rudiments of Latin and English Grammar; By the late Alexander Adam, L.L.D. Second New York, from the Ninth English Edition, New-York: Published by Evert Duyckinck, and George Long. 1820 (?).

HM945, A.

6. Greek Grammar from the German of Philip Buttman. Second edition of the Translation. Boston: Cummings, Hilliard, and Company. 1826.

HER; *HM945*, A: Thoreau's copy is now in the possession of the Concord Free Public Library. The flyleaf bears the autograph "D. H. Thoreau Cambridge Mass 1833." This edition was translated into English by Edward Everett and edited by George Bancroft, later famous for his ten-volume *History of the United States*, and by George H. Bode, a German classicist whose chief interest was in the mystic writings.

7. Quinti Horatii Flacci Opera. Cura B. A. Gould, A.M. Bostoniae; Hilliard, Gray, Little et Wilkins 1828.

HCI; HBA; *HM945*, A: This is the only first-year Harvard text which appears on the *Index Rerum* list. Thoreau also owned another edition of Horace. One or the other of these books was owned by F. H. Bigelow in 1872.

8. The Orations of Aeschines and Demosthenes on the Crown. By Alexander Negris. Boston: Hilliard, Gray, Little, and Wilkins. 1829.

HCI; PC, p. 94: This is one of the specific items on Sanborn's reading list (*Henry David Thoreau*, pp. 520–1). According to the annual presidential report in the Harvard College catalogue, only advanced scholars among the freshmen read both Aeschines and Demosthenes. Negris was a native Greek and a minor classical scholar.

9. Titi Livii Patavini Historiarum Liber Primus et Selecta Quaedam Capita. Carolus Folsom, A.M., Academiae Harvardianae olim Bibliothecarius Cantabrigiae: Hilliard et Brown. 1829 (?).

HCI; PC, p. 90. This is a freshman text.

10. ΞΕΝΟΦΩΝΤΟΣ ΑΝΑΒΑΣΙΣ ΚΥΡΟΥ. Xenophon's Expedition of Cyrus, with English Notes, by Charles Dexter Cleveland, Professor of Languages in Dickinson College. Boston: Hilliard, Gray, and Company 1830.

HCI; PC, p. 93. This is also a freshman text.

11. An Epitome of Grecian Antiquities. by Charles D. Cleveland. Boston: Hilliard, Gray, Little, and Wilkins: and Richardson and Lord. 1827 (?).

HCI; HBA: Thoreau withdrew a copy of this book from the Harvard College library on February 12, 1834 (Cameron, II, 192, 200). This text emphasizes government, military affairs, religion, and learning, and minimizes daily life and customs. It is a good reference book, documentary rather than discursive in style. It was studied by freshmen and sophomores.

12. Roman Antiquities: By Alexander Adam, L.L.D. Revised, corrected, and illustrated with notes and additions, by P. Wilson, L.L.D. with additional notes, by L. L. da Ponte, New-York: Collins and Hannay; Collins and Co.; and N. and J. White. 1833.

HCI; HPR: This is a text like Cleveland's *Epitome* in style; it is heavily documented, the kind of book from which a student would learn a great deal or a very little. It has one section of special interest on agriculture and husbandry, annotated with references to Varro, Cato, Columella, and Palladius. This could be the source of Thoreau's interest in the husbandry writers. The book also has a philological bias. It was studied by freshmen and sophomores.

13. A Grammar of the Greek Language. by Benjamin Franklin Fisk. Second Edition. Boston: Hilliard, Gray, Little, and Wilkins. M DCCC XXXI (?).

HCI; PC, p. 92: This was used throughout the entire classical course at Harvard.

14. Greek Exercises; By Benjamin Franklin Fisk. Boston: Hilliard, Gray, Little, and Wilkins 1831 (?).

HCI; PC, p. 91: This was used with the Fisk grammar through all three years of the classical course. Thoreau withdrew a copy of this book from the Harvard College library on February 5, 1834 (Cameron, II, 192, 201).

15. A Grammar of the Latin Language, From the German of C. G. Zumpt. New-York: G. & C. Carvill, 108 Broadway, 1829.

HCI; HPR: This text was used by freshmen and sophomores. Thoreau used the first American edition, following seven German and two English editions. The editor was historian George Bancroft.

16. Medea, a Tragedy of Seneca. Edited by Charles Beck, Professor of Latin in Harvard University. Cambridge and Boston: James Munroe & Co., Booksellers to the University. 1834.

HPR; *HM945*, A: Thoreau, as a sophomore, studied this text under its editor, a German scholar who came to the United States in 1824. Thoreau's copy was in the possession of F. H. Bigelow in 1872.

17. 'ΟΜΗΡΟΥ 'ΙΛΙΑΣ. The Iliad of Homer, from the text of Wolf with English notes, and Flaxman's Designs. Edited By C. C. Felton, A.M., Eliot Professor of Greek in Harvard University. Second Edition. Boston: Hilliard, Gray, and Company. 1834.

HCI; PC, p. 52; *HM945*, A: Thoreau, as a junior, studied this text under the man who prepared it. A Latin summary of each book of the *Iliad* is provided.

18. D. Junii Juvenalis Satirae Expurgatae. cura F. P. Leverett. Bostoniae: Hilliard, Gray, Little, et Wilkins. 1828.

HCI; PC, p. 91: Thoreau read this as a junior. Prepared by Leverett of the Boston Latin School for his pupils, it was popular enough to be adopted on the college level. It was particularly advertised as expurgated.

19. Grecian Antiquities; By the Rev. Thomas Harwood, London: 1801.

This was not a college text. Thoreau withdrew this book from the Harvard College library on January 29, 1834 (Cameron, II, 192, 202).

20. Graecum Lexicon Manuale primum a Benjamine Hederico institutum Editio nova Petri Henr. Larcheri. Londini 1821.

Thoreau did not own this dictionary. He withdrew it from the Harvard College library on October 28, 1834 (Cameron, II, 193, 202).

21. Alcestis Euripidea. edidit Gottlob Adolph Wagner. Lipsiae sumtibus Engelh. Beniam. Suicquerti. cıɔıɔccc.

Thoreau withdrew this book from the Harvard College library on February 10, 1835 (Cameron, II, 193, 201) when he was reading the *Alcestis* in class during his sophomore year. In this edition the *Alcestis* is bound with the *Ion;* it is not known whether Thoreau read the *Ion.*

22. Joan. Scapulae Lexicon Graeco-Latinum, Editio nova accurata. Lugduni Batavorum, Typis Bonaventurae & Abraham Elzeviriorum, E Francisci Hackii. M. DC. LII.

Thoreau withdrew this Greek-Latin lexicon from the Harvard College library on June 9, 1835 (Cameron, II, 193, 207).

23. Homeri Ilias C. G. Heyne Lipsiae 1804.

Thoreau withdrew this book from the Harvard College library on September 3, 1835 (Cameron, II, 193, 203) when he was studying the *Iliad* in his junior year. The Heyne text is a famous and scholarly one.

24. The Iliads and Odysses of Homer. Translated out of Greek into English. by Tho: Hobbes of Malmsbury. The Second Edition. London: Printed for Will. Crook, at the green Dragon without Temple-Barre. 1677.

Thoreau also withdrew this seventeenth-century English translation of Homer from the Harvard College library during his junior year on April 28, 1836 (Cameron, II, 193, 203).

25. Introductions to the study of the Greek Classic Poets. by Henry Nelson Coleridge, Esq. M.A. Part I. London: MDCCCXXX.

Thoreau withdrew a third book relating to Homer from the Harvard College library on September 15, 1836 (Cameron, II, 193, 200). He wrote a review of the book, possibly for a class exercise. The review is No. 7 of a group of similar exercises in the Huntington Library manuscript *HM934*.

26. Cornelii Nepotis vitae Excellentium Imperatorum: Cum versione Anglica, By John Clarke. The Tenth Edition. London, M.DCC.LXV.

Thoreau withdrew this from the Harvard College library during his senior year on June 26, 1837 (Cameron, II, 194, 206), when he was no longer studying the classics. He used the book for writing a theme, "Titus Pomponicus Atticus as an Example" (Sanborn, *Henry David Thoreau,* pp. 183–5), quoting from Nepos both in Latin and in English. Nepos' *Lives* also appears on Sanborn's reading list (*Henry David Thoreau,* pp. 520–1). The general entry is followed by a list of eight names: Miltiades, Themistocles, Aristides, Alcibiades, Epaminondas, Phocion, Hannibal, and Cato Major. Such specification seems to guarantee reading. It is peculiar that Atticus is not included in the list.

27. D. Junii Juvenalis et A. Persii Flacci satirae. in usum serenissimi delphini. Ed. prima Americana. Philadelphiae, impensis M. Carey, 1814.

HM945, A: This seems to be the only American Delphine edition of Juvenal and Persius combined. I have taken the bibliographical data from the listing of the catalogue of the Library of Congress.

28. Publii Ovidii Nasonis Metamorphoseon Libri xv. in usum Serenissimi Delphini. Novi-Eboraci: Impensis George Long et Thomas De Silver, Philadelphiae. 1823 (?).

HM945, A: There were Delphine editions of Ovid published in Philadelphia in 1805 and 1817; Thoreau might have had one of these earlier editions.

29. Plutarch's Lives, Translated From the original Greek; By John Langhorne, D.D. and William Langhorne, A.M.

HM945, A: The Langhorne translation was published in many editions by many firms. I have not been able to determine publisher or date and have given only a description common to all editions.

30. ΞΕΝΟΦΩΝΤΟΣ ΚΥΡΟΥ ΠΑΙΔΕΙΑΣ ΒΙΒΛΙΑ ΟΚΤΩ Xenophontis De Cyri Institutione Libri Octo. Thomas Hutchinson, A.M. Editio prima Americana: Cura Johannis Watts. Philadelphiae: Impensis Wm. Poyntell et Soc. 1806.

HM945, A: Sanborn lists this book (*Henry David Thoreau,* p. 508) correctly except for spelling.

31. Curtius Rufus, Quintus. Historia Alexandri Magni. Ed. stereotypa ex

nova tabularum impressione emendatissima. Lipsiae, sumtibus et typis C. Tauchnitii, 1829.

HM945, A: The bibliographical data is from the catalogue of the Library of Congress. This book, with the Plutarch, and Xenophon's *Anabasis* and *Cyropaedia* probably provided both the source and the satisfaction of Thoreau's interest in Alexander. It was owned by F. H. Bigelow in 1872.

32. An abridgement of Ainsworth's dictionary, English and Latin, By Thomas Morell, D.D. Carefully corrected and improved from the last London quarto edition by John Carey, LL.D. Philadelphia. 1829 (?).

HM945, A: The listing is from the catalogue of the Library of Congress. Thoreau could have had an 1831 edition.

33. A Greek and English Lexicon; Second edition, Boston: Hilliard, Gray, Little, and Wilkins. 1829 (?).

HM945, A: This is Pickering's Greek-English adaptation of the Greek-Latin Schrevelius. Thoreau could have had the first edition of 1826.

34. A Classical dictionary; By J. Lemprière, D.D. First American from the sixth London edition. New-York. 1809 (?).

HM945, A: I have given the first American edition; there were at least six before 1836. Lemprière has consistently maintained its original popularity; the most recent edition came out in 1949. Thoreau's copy of the book was given by Sophia to a Mr. Calvin Greene of Rochester, Michigan. (Jones, S. A., *Some Unpublished Letters of Henry D. and Sophia E. Thoreau* [New York, The Marian Press, 1899], prefatory note, p. xi.)

35. P. Virgilii Maronis Opera, Chr. G. Heyne, Londini: Excudit T. Davison. 1822.

HM945, B: This was Thoreau's second Vergil text. It was owned by F. H. Bigelow in 1872.

36. Plutarch's Morals: Translated from the Greek, By Several Hands. The Fifth Edition. London, 1718.

College Note-Book (*MA. 594*), pp. 76ʳ–76ᵛ, contains quotations from No. 36, 11, 371, 409, 454, 463–4. The Fruitlands library had the third edition of this book, but I have listed the fifth for two reasons: it is not likely that Thoreau could have had access to the Fruitlands book this early, and the very strange capitalization in his extracts does not at all agree with that of the third edition and does very nearly agree with that of the fifth edition.

37. ΠΙΝΔΑΡΟΣ. Pindari Olympia, Pythia, Nemea, Isthmia. Graece & Latine, Apud Hieronymum Commelinum, Elect. Palat. typographum. Anno cIɔ Iɔ xciix.

HM945, C: Sanborn says that Thoreau's copy came from the Fruitlands library (*Henry David Thoreau*, p. 506). Further evidence is the Henry Stephanus translation of Anacreon's "On the Rose" in *A Book of Extracts*, p. 228. Edited by Henry Stephanus or Henri Estienne, the book was annotated by Portus for the Commelin Press in Heidelberg. It includes the Pindaric odes and fragments and the poems of many other Greek poets. It is a rare and interesting book.

38. ΟΡΦΕΩS ΑΡΓΟΝΑΥΤΙΚΑ ΥΜΝΟΙ ΚΑΙ ΠΕΡΙ ΛΙΘΩΝ Orphei Argonautica et de lapidibus Accedunt Henrici Stephani in omnia & Josephi Sca-

ligeri in Hymnos Notae. Trajecti ad Rhenum. Apud Guilelmum vande Water. CIƆ IƆ CLXXXIX.

HM945, C: This appears on the *Index Rerum* list between Nos. 37 and 40 and has the same very simple listing which they have, the result probably of difficulty in reducing the old title pages to any standard form. Sanborn includes it among the Fruitlands books (*Henry David Thoreau,* p. 506). For all these reasons I have so identified it. Thoreau did not, however, use this Orpheus for the selections which he copied into the *Literary Note-Book,* and I have been unable to locate any text from which they came.

39. Orpheus Poetarum Graecorum Antiquissimus. Auctore Georgio Henrico Bode. Gottingae typis Dieterichianis. MDCCCXXIV.

This appears on a reading list in *HM13201* with the date April 15, 1841, and the parenthetical comment "partially." Quotations from all other entries on this reading list appear in the *Literary Note-Book;* there is none from this. This is, however, not a test of Orpheus but a discussion of Orphic history and tradition. The specification "partially" suggests that Thoreau at least examined, if he did not read, the book.

40. Poetae Minores Graeci. Fragmenta Quaedam Accedunt etiam Observationes Radulphi Wintertoni in Hesiodum, Cantabrigiae, Ex Officina Joan. Hayes, Celeberrimae Academicae Typographi. MDCLXXVII.

HM945, C: Thoreau identifies this as the Fruitlands copy (*Writings,* VI, 60; letter to Emerson, February 15, 1843). Sanborn (*Henry David Thoreau,* p. 506) includes it among the Fruitlands books. It contains poems of forty-five Greek poets. There is a Latin version of the Greek text.

41. Jamblichus' Life of Pythagoras, Translated from the Greek. By Thomas Taylor. London: 1818.

This book appears on the reading list in *HM13201* under the date of April 15, 1841. The *Literary Note-Book* identifies it as Taylor's translation. There are, however, in this commonplace book some extracts which do not come from Taylor and which I have been unable to trace to any source. The book does not appear on the *Index Rerum* list nor among the Harvard borrowings. It may possibly have belonged to Emerson.

42. Select Works of Porphyry; Translated from the Greek by Thomas Taylor. London: 1823.

This appears on the *HM13201* reading list of April 15, 1841.

43. A Copious and Critical Latin-English Lexicon, By E. A. Andrews, LL.D. New York; Harper & Brothers, Publishers. 1856 (?).

IR, C: There are a number of editions both before and after this. I have made an arbitrary choice.

44. A Dictionary of Select and Popular Quotations, By D. E. Macdonnel, First American from the fifth London Edition, Philadelphia. 1810.

HM945, C: Thoreau's copy is now in the possession of the Concord Free Public Library. The autograph "Eliza Thoreau" appears on the title page and "D. Thoreau" appears on the front flyleaf. The quotations are preponderantly although not exclusively Latin and Greek.

45. Oswald (John) An Etymological Dictionary of the English Language, Philadelphia, 1844.

HM945, C: This book was once in the possession of the Concord Free

Public Library according to the Wakeman collection catalogue, from which the bibliographical data given here is taken (Item 1063). It is not properly a dictionary, but a treatise on the classical derivation of English words. For Thoreau's mention of the book see *Writings,* xv, 138; November, 1856.

46. Mystagogus Poeticus, Or The Muses Interpreter: By Alexander Ross. London, M.DC.XLVIII(?).

Thoreau mentions this book in *Writings,* vii, 392, and draws material from it for *ibid.,* vii, 391–4, and i, 58–9. It is a curious little book, attempting to interpret classical mythology in terms of universal truth. I have listed the second edition simply because I had access to it. Editions 3–6 appeared in 1653, 1664, 1672, and 1675.

47. Rei Rusticae Auctores Latini Veteres M. Cato M. Varro L. Columella Palladius Ex Hier. Commelini typographio, Anno MDXCV.

This is Alcott's copy of the Sylburgius edition of the husbandry writers. Alcott lent it to Thoreau in 1851 (Shepard, *The Journals of Bronson Alcott,* p. 253, entry of August 11, 1851). Thoreau kept it at least until 1856 when he was comparing it with an English edition of Columella (*Manuscript Journals [MA. 1302]*). The book is still in possession of the Alcott family; Frederic Wolsey Pratt, the present owner, furnished me with the bibliographical description.

48. ΣΟΦΟΚΛΕΟΥΣ ΑΝΤΙΓΟΝΗ. The Antigone of Sophocles in Greek and English; by John William Donaldson, B.D., London: John W. Parker, West Strand. M. DCCC. XLVIII.

This was withdrawn from the Harvard College library on September 4, 1855 (Cameron, ii, 197, 207).

49. L. Junius Moderatus Columella of Husbandry, in Twelve Books: and his Book concerning Trees. Translated into English, London: Printed for A. Miller, opposite to Catherine-street in the Strand M.DCC. XLV.

Thoreau withdrew this from the Harvard College library on March 4, 1856 (Cameron, ii, 197, 200).

50. ΘΕΟΦΡΑΣΤΟΥ ΕΡΕΣΙΟΥ ΤΑ ΣΩΖΟΜΕΝΑ Theophrasti Eresii quae supersunt opera et excerpta librorum quatuor tomis comprehensa. ad fidem librorum editorum et scriptorum emendavit Historiam et libros vi de caus is plantarum coniuncta opera D. H. F. Linkii excerpta. solus explicare conatus est Io. Gottlob Schneider, saxo. Lipsiae 1818 sumtibus Frid. Christ. Guil. Vogelii.

Thoreau withdrew the second volume of this work from the Harvard College library on December 16, 1859 (Cameron, ii, 198, 208). He copied selections from it into *A Book of Extracts,* pp. 138–45, giving adequate bibliographical identification. The text is given both in Greek and in Latin.

51. Histoire des Animaux d'Aristote, Avec la Traduction Française, *Par* M. Camus, A Paris, Chez la Veuve Desaint, Libraire, rue du Foin S. Jacques. M DCC LXXXIII.

Thoreau withdrew both volumes of this work from the Harvard College library on December 16, 1859 (Cameron, ii, 198, 199). He copied from this into *A Book of Extracts,* pp. 78 ff., giving adequate bibliographical identification of source.

52. ΚΛ. ΑΙΛΙΑΝΟΥ ΣΟΦΙΣΤΟΥ ΠΟΙΚΙΛΗΣ ΙΣΤΟΡΙΑΣ βιβλία ιΔ Cl. Ae-

liani Sophistae Variae Historiae Libri xiv. cum notis Johannis Schefferi, interpretatione Justi Vulteii, annotationibusque Joachimi Kühnii. Editio postrema curante John. Henrico Lederlino. Anno m dc xiii.

Cameron (ii, 198) says that Thoreau withdrew an edition of Aelian from the Harvard College library on February 6, 1860, but fails to identify it from the library records. It can be identified as this edition from *A Book of Extracts,* pp. 186–7.

53. ΑΙΛΙΑΝΟΥ ΠΕΡΙ ΖΩΩΝ ΙΔΙΟΤΗΤΟΣ βιβλια ιz Aeliani de Natura Animalium Libri xvii. graece et latine edidit Io. Gottlob Schneider. Lipsiae sumtibus E. B. Schwickerti. mdcclxxxiv.

Thoreau withdrew this book from the Harvard College Library on April 9, 1860 (Cameron, ii, 198). He neither mentioned it nor quoted from it.

54. The Natural History of Pliny. Translated, by the late John Bostock, M.D., F.R.S. and H. T. Riley, Esq., B.A., London: Henry G. Bohn, York Street, Covent Garden. mdccclv.

Thoreau listed "Pliny in Bohn's Library" in the back of the *Harvard Fact-Book* among other books which he wanted to consult. Bohn had an extensive list of cheap classical translations. Thoreau made extracts from the Bohn Pliny in *A Book of Extracts,* pp. 128–37, 146–60, 282. The extracts are paged with reference to this edition as well as to another edition of Pliny which Thoreau owned (Supplement to Appendix A, No. 14).

55. Herodotus, a new and literal version From the text of Baehr. By Henry Cary, M.A., London: Henry G. Bohn, York Street, Covent Garden: mdcccliv.

Excerpts from this edition of Herodotus appear in *A Book of Extracts,* pp. 256–64. The source is given by Thoreau as "Herodotus—Cary's trans. in Bohn's Series."

Supplement to Appendix A

NOTE: Here I have listed works or authors which there is reason to believe Thoreau read but which I have not been able to identify adequately. They are given in generally chronological order and are followed by whatever information I have found about them.

1. Caesar
HM945, A: "Caesaris Commentarii Lipsiae ed 1 v." This may have been an elementary or academy text, or it may possibly have belonged originally to another member of the Thoreau family.

2. Sallust
HER: "some Sallust." I have found no evidence that Thoreau read Sallust.

3. Greek Testament
HER: the four gospels of the Greek Testament; *HM945,* A: "Greek Testament—Worcester? 1 v." I have not been able to identify this dubiously recorded entry. Harvard used an edition of Griesbach at that time.

4. Cicero's *De claris oratoribus*
PC, p. 85: This is listed as one of a series of classics used at Harvard. It

was certainly locally prepared, but no editor is named. I have been unable to find the 1833 edition of this, but a later edition names Charles Beck as editor. The text sold for twenty cents.

5. Cicero's *De officiis*

This is another of the series to which No. 4 above belonged. It would be a reasonable guess that Beck edited it also. It sold for thirty-three cents.

6. Sophocles' *Tragedies*

HCI: Sophomores were required to read *Oedipus Tyrannus, Oedipus Colonus,* and *Antigone.* There seem to have been no school texts of Greek tragedy available at this time. Shattuck, Brown, and Company had one in press but it was not on the market until too late for Thoreau's use; *HM945,* A: "Sophoclis Tragoed—Lipsiae ed. 1 v." This seems to be a Tauchnitz text, but I could not determine edition or date of publication. The book was owned by F. H. Bigelow in 1872.

7. Euripides' *Tragedies*

HCI: Sophomores were required to read *Alcestis; HM945,* A: "Euripidis Tragoediae—Lipsiae ed. 4 v. in 2." Sanborn has misprinted this (*Henry David Thoreau,* p. 507), substituting the words "in 1858" from another line for the correct words "4 v. in 2"; the manuscript is perfectly clear. Again, this seems to be a Tauchnitz text of unidentifiable edition and date. Bigelow owned the book in 1872.

8. Horace

HM945, A: "Horatius—Ex ed. J. C. Zeunii, Londini—Nova-Eboraci 1 v." I have found London Zeunii editions in 1822 and 1825, but no London-New York edition. F. H. Bigelow owned either this or the Gould Horace (App. A. No. 7) in 1872. Thoreau seems to have used this text instead of the Gould in his quotations from Horace.

9. Dryden's Virgil

HM945, A: "Dryden's Virgil—Philad. ed. 2. v." I have found only one two-volume edition of Dryden's Vergil, published by Sorin and Ball sometime between 1820 and 1852. (O. A. Roorbach, *Catalogue of American Publications from 1820–1852,* New York, O. A. Roorbach, 1852). These two volumes were given to Elizabeth Weir after Thoreau's death.

10. Pope's *Works*

HM945, B: "Pope's Works 5. v." At the right of this entry has been scrawled in pencil "2d. stolen." This was probably the volume of Pope's Homer which Thoreau tells us (*Writings,* II, 191) was stolen from his table at Walden. I have been unable to identify the edition of Pope.

11. Aeschylus

On the evidence of the journal, Thoreau began to read *Prometheus Bound* in November, 1839 (*Writings,* VII, 94). The translation was published in the *Dial* for January, 1843. On August 7, 1843, Thoreau wrote to Emerson from New York (*ibid.,* VI, 102) that he had made "a very rude translation of the Seven against Thebes." Apparently Thoreau never owned a copy of Aeschylus, and I have been unable to find either in Concord or New York any record of his borrowing one.

12. Long's Classical Atlas

HM945, C: "Long's Classical Atlas 1 v." The only edition of this that I can locate is a New York, 1870, edition showing a copyright by Blanchard and Lee, Philadelphia, in 1856.

13. Lucretius

See *Writings,* XIV, 312.

14. Pliny's *Historiae Mundi*

HM945, C: "Plinii Hist. 3 vols. 1593." Thoreau's copy was given by Sophia to H. G. O. Blake. It was extant in 1924 when it was listed as Item 1054 in the Wakeman Collection catalogue with the additional identification "Apud Jacobum Stoer." This was the last classical acquisition that Thoreau made for his own library.

15. Strabo

See *Writings,* VI, 379, April 10, 1861; XX, 338, n. 2, in which Thoreau identifies the book as a Bohn publication.

16. Aesop

See *Writings,* III, 90, 469.

17. Tacitus

Thoreau translates and quotes from the last two chapters of Tacitus' *Agricola* in *Writings,* IV, 452–4. The use of this material in funeral eulogies was so common that I suspect Thoreau read no more of Tacitus. The quotation in "Wild Apples" is almost certainly secondary.

APPENDIX B

CLASSICAL QUOTATIONS IN THOREAU

Prefatory Note

IN THIS appendix I have listed and identified Thoreau's quotations from the major classical authors which he read. I have included with the quotations any references which are so specific as to be subject to line location. This I have done in an effort to give a comprehensive picture of Thoreau's reading and interest in each author. I have omitted certain classical material not indicative of classical reading: secondhand quotation such as Aristotle in Humboldt or Pliny in Gesner; Greek and Latin quotations taken from collections of quotation; and fragments of classical writing in popular use in certain established contexts, such as the closing portion of Tacitus' *Agricola* as funeral eulogy or monumental inscription. No attempt has been made to identify quotations of two or three words only, unless they are so well known and so individual as to be immediately referred to one and only one source. Authors from whom Thoreau quoted only a few times have not been listed in this appendix but have been included in Appendix C.

Because of the technical difficulties of dealing with manuscript material, the collection of quotation and reference has been restricted to the published works except in two cases. The Horace and Persius material comes almost entirely from manuscript; its omission would be misleading. The quotation from the husbandry writers which appears in the manuscript journals, however, adds nothing but bulk to the treatment and has, therefore, been excluded.

Authors are arranged alphabetically. Under each author the order of arrangement is chronological. Quotation is given according to Thoreau rather than from classical text.

Cato

NOTE: Each passage is preceded by notation indicating its location in Thoreau's writing and its classical source. References before the colon are to *Writings;* identifications after the colon are from Cato's *De agri cultura.* The first number of the identification is for chapter; the second, where a second is required, for section. The passages are taken as they occur in Thoreau; all variations from standard text are referable to him. Since I have no copy of the edition in which he read the rustic writers, I cannot say whether variations are actually attributable to him or to the edition of Cato which he used.

II, 70 (*Walden;* 1845–54) : 74

Panem depsticium sic facito. Manus mortarium bene lavato. Farinam in mortarium indito, aquae paulatim addito, subigitoque pulchre. Ubi bene subegeris, defingito, coquitoque sub testu."[1]

1. Thoreau gives an English translation of this passage.

II, 93 (*Walden;* 1845–54) : 1, 1

"When you think of getting a farm turn it thus in your mind, not to buy greedily; nor spare your pains to look at it, and do not think it enough to go round it once. The oftener you go there the more it will please you, if it is good."

II, 180 (*Walden;* 1845–54) : 2, 7

. . . (patrem familias vendacem, non emacem esse oportet)[2]

II, 183 (*Walden;* 1845–54) : introduction, 4

. . . (*maximeque pius quaestus*) . . .[3]

II, 268 (*Walden;* 1845–54) : 3, 2

Cato says, the master of a family (*patremfamilias*) must have in his rustic villa "cellam oleariam, vinariam, dolia multa, ubi lubeat caritatem expectare, et rei, et virtuti, et gloriae erit."[4]

II, 276–7 (Walden; 1845–54) : 139

I would that our farmers when they cut down a forest felt some of that awe which the old Romans did when they came to thin, or let in the light to, a consecrated grove (*lucum conlucare*), that is, would believe that it is sacred to some god. The Romans made an expiatory offering, and prayed, Whatever god or goddess thou art to whom this grove is sacred, be propitious to me, my family, and children, etc.[5]

VIII, 445; September 2, 1851 : 5, 8; 6, 1

"Sterquilinium magnum stude ut habeas. Stercus sedulo conserva, cum exportabis purgato et comminuito. Per autumnum evehito."[6]

They [Romans] [7] planted *rapa, raphanos, milium* and *panicum* in low foggy land, *ager nebulosus.*

VIII, 446; September 2, 1851 : 5, 8

The *faenum cordum,* the aftermath, *sicilimenta de prato,* the second mowings of the meadow, this reminds me of, in Cato.

2. This appears in *Writings,* VIII, 442–3; September 2, 1851, thus: *"Patremfamilias vendacem, non emacem esse oportet."*

3. This is amplified in *ibid.,* XII, 106–7; February 8, 1854, to include most of the introduction: "Et virum bonum cum laudabant, bonum agricolam, bonumque colonum. Amplissime laudari existabatur, qui ita laudabatur. Mercatorem autem strenuum studiosumque rei querendae existimo; verum . . . periculosum et calamitosum. At ex agricolis et viri fortissimi, et milites strenuissimi gignuntur, maximeque pius quaestus, stabilissimusque consequitur, minimeque invidiosus: minimeque male cogitantes sunt, qui in eo studio occupati sunt." (introd., 2, 3, 4.) Thoreau gives the English translation also. He refers to the passage again in *Writings,* VIII, 450; September 3, 1851.

4. The same selection is quoted in *Writings,* XII, 69; January 14, 1854. In both cases the passage is followed by an English translation. The passage is referred to again, *ibid.,* VIII, 446; September 2, 1851.

5. This is repeated with variation in *ibid.,* XII, 72–3.

6. Thoreau gives an English translation.

7. The brackets are mine.

VIII, 450 ; September 3, 1851 : 2, 4

> . . . as Cato says, *per ferias potuisse fossas veteres tergeri,* that in the holidays old ditches might have been cleaned out.

IX, 61 ; October 9, 1851 : 5, 7 ; 6, 3

> "Stramenta si deerunt, frondem iligneam legito, eam substernito ovibus bubusque."[8]

> "Circum vias ulmos serito, et partim populos, uti frondem ovibus et bubus habeas."[9]

XII, 68–9 ; January 14, 1854 : 1, 7 ; 7, 1

> Cato makes the vineyard of first importance to a farm; second, a well-watered garden; third, a willow plantation (*salictum*) ; fourth, an olive-yard (oletum) ; fifth, a meadow or grass ground (?) (*pratum*) ; sixth, a grain-field or tillage (?) (*campus frumentarius*) ; seventh, a copse-wood (?) for fuel (?)[1] (silva caedua) . . . eighth, an arbustum . . . (*arbustum*) ; ninth, a wood that yields mast (*glandaria silva*). He says elsewhere the *arbustum* yields *ligna et virgae.*

XII, 69 ; January 14, 1854 : 3, 1 ; 3, 2 ; 5, 3

> "In earliest manhood the master of a family must study to plant his ground; as for building he must think a long time about it (*diu cogitare*) ; he must not think about planting, but do it. When he gets to be thirty-six years old, then let him build, if he has his ground planted. So build, that the village may not have to seek the farm, nor the farm the villa."

> This, too, to make farmers prudent and thrifty: "Cogitato quotannis tempestates magnas venire, et oleam dejicere solere" (Consider that great tempests come every year, and the olive is wont to fall). The steward must not lend seed for sowing, etc. He may have two or three families of whom to borrow and to whom to lend and no more.

XII, 71 ; January 14, 1854 : 5, 7 ; 6, 4 ; 6, 1 ; 23, 2 ; 54, 5

> "If you have done one thing late, you will do all your work late," says Cato to the farmer. They raised a sallow (*salicem*) to tie vines with. Ground subject to fog is called *nebulosus.* They made a cheap wine of poor grapes, called *vinum praeliganeum,* for the laborers to drink.

> Oxen "must have muzzles [or little baskets, *fiscellas*],[2] that they may not go in quest of grass (*ne herbam sectentur*) when they plow."

XII, 71 ; January 17, 1854 : 73

> Cato, prescribing a *medicamentum* for oxen, says, "When you see

8. Thoreau gives an English translation for this.

9. There is a reflection of these passages in *Writings,* IX, 63, where, speaking of leaves, Thoreau asks, "Might we not fill beds with them or use them for fodder or litter?"

1. In the husbandry writers Thoreau frequently questions his translation of a word. This is not to be wondered at; reading the husbandry writers requires a new technical vocabulary.

2. The journal editors assign these brackets to Thoreau.

a snake's slough, take it and lay it up, that you may not have to seek it when it is wanted." This was mixed with bread, corn, etc.

XII, 71–2; January 17, 1854: 75–9; 83

He tells how to make bread and different kinds of cakes, *viz.,* a *libum,* a *placenta,* a *spira* (so called because twisted like a rope, perhaps like doughnuts), *scriblita* (because ornamented with characters like writing), *globi* (globes), etc., etc. Tells how to make a vow for your oxen to Mars Sylvanus in a wood with an offering, no woman to be present nor know how it is done.

XII, 72; January 17, 1854: 88, 2; 89; 110; 111; 124; 131; 132

When the brine will float a dry *maena* (a fish) or an egg, then it will preserve meat. Tells how to cram hens and geese. If you wish to remove an ill savor from wine, he recommends to heat a brick and pitch it and let it down by a string to the bottom of the cask and there remain two days, the cask being stopped.

"If you wish to know if water has been added to wine, make a little vessel of ivy wood (*materia ederacea*). Put into it the wine which you think has water in it. If it has water, the wine will run out (*effluet*), the water will remain. For a vessel of ivy wood does not hold wine."

"The dogs must be shut up by day that they may be more sharp (*acriores,* more fierce (?)) and vigilant by night."

"Make a sacrificial feast for the oxen when the pear is in blossom. Afterward begin to plow in the spring."

"That day is to be holy (*feriae*) to the oxen, and herdsmen, and those who make the feast." They offer wine and mutton to Jupiter Dapalis, also to Vesta if they choose.

XII, 73; January 17, 1854: 141; 160

A *lustrum,* or sacrifice, of a sow, sheep, and bull (*suovitaurilia*) was performed every fifth year, when various things were prayed for.[3]

Gives several charms to cure diseases, mere magician's words.

Columella

NOTE: The references before the colon are to Thoreau's *Writings;* the identifications after the colon are from Columella's *De re rustica.* The first number is for book; the second, for chapter. Since the sections within the chapters given in a modern standard text differ from those in the English Columella which Thoreau read, I have given no section numbers. I have, however, given pagination for Thoreau's edition of Columella.

3. The information that the *lustrum* was performed every fifth year is not in Cato, but it is in Lemprière.

XII, 69; January 13, 1854: iii, 2 (p. 110)

(Columella says it [an arbustum]⁴ is a plantation of elms, etc., for vines to rest on)

XII, 111; February 9, 1854: i, preface (p. 7)

Columella, referring to Varro, gives the same reason for the setting aside of the ninth day only, and adds: "Illis enim temporibus proceres civitatis in agris morabantur; et cum consilium publicum desiderabatur, a villis arcessebantur in senatum. Ex quo qui eos evocabant, Viatores nominati sunt . . ."⁵

XII, 112–13; February 9, 1854: i, preface (pp. 5–6)

The illustrious farmer Romans who lived simply on their land, to whom Columella refers, are Q. Cincinnatus, C. Fabricius, and Curius Dentatus.

XII, 125; February 16, 1854: i, 1 (pp. 15–18)

Columella, after saying that many authors had believed that the climate ("qualitatem caeli statumque") was changed by lapse of time ("longo aevi situ"), refers to Hipparchus as having given out that the time would be when the poles of the earth would be moved from their place ("tempus fore, quo cardines mundi loco moverentur"); and, as confirmatory of this, he (C.) goes on to say that the vine and olive flourish now in some places where formerly they failed.

He gives the names of about fifty authors who had treated *de rusticis rebus* before him.

XIV, 52; December 17, 1855: i, 6 (p. 37)

Columella says you must be careful not to carry out seeds in your manure and so have *segetes herbidas* (weedy crops).

XIV, 56–7; December 22, 1855: i, 3 (p. 25)

Modus ergo, qui in omnibus rebus, etiam parandis agris adhibebitur: tantum enim obtinendum est, quanto est opus, ut emisse videamur quo potiremur, non quo oneraremur ipsi, atque aliis fruendum eriperemus, more praepotentium, qui possident fines gentium, quos ne circumire equis quidem valent, sed proculcandos pecudibus, et vastandos ac populandos feris derelinquunt, aut occupatos nexu civium, et ergastulis tenent."⁶

XIV, 312; April 26, 1856: ii, 22 (pp. 101–2)

"But the custom of our ancestors also permitted these things on holidays: to pound wheat, cut torches, make candles, cultivate a hired vineyard, clear out and purge fish-ponds, ponds, and old ditches, mow grass ground a second time, spread dung, store up hay on scaffolds, gather the fruit of a hired olive yard, spread apples, pears, and figs, make cheese, bring home trees for the sake of planting on our shoulders or on a pack-mule, but not with one harnessed to a cart, nor to plant them when brought

---

4. The bracketed insertion is mine.
5. The English translation is included as a part of the quotation.
6. Thoreau gives an English translation.

home, nor to open the ground, nor prune a tree, not even to attend to sowing seed, unless you have first sacrificed a puppy."

xiv, 329–30; May 11, 1856: i, 4–5, *passim* (pp. 25–31)

The Roman writers Columella and Palladius warn not to build in a low valley or by a marsh, and the same rule is observed here to-day.

Homer

NOTE: References before the colon are to Thoreau's *Writings;* all identifications are from the *Iliad* unless otherwise indicated. Thoreau's quotations, compared with the Felton edition which he used, show several minor variations and inaccuracies.

vii, 31 ; March 3, 1838 : i, 47 ; i, 104

—'οδ' ἤιε νυκτὶ 'εοικως

—ὄσσε δέ οξ πυρὶ λαωπετόωντε ἐίκτην,—

vii, 31–2; March 4, 1838: i, 259–63[7]

"But you are younger than I. For time was when I conversed with greater men than you. For not at any time have I seen such men, nor shall see them, as Perithous and Dryas and ποιμένα λαῶν."

vii, 33 ; March 4, 1838: i, 156–7

'επειὴ μάλα πολλὰ μεταξύ
Οὔρεά τε σκιόεντα, θάλασσά τε ἠχήεσσα,—[8]

vii, 33 ; March 5, 1838: i, 189; i, 196[9]

διάνδιχα μερμήριξεν (of Achilles)

θυμῷ φιλέουσά τε, κηδομένη τε (of Pallas Athene)[1]

vii, 33 ; March 5, 1838: i, 247–9

"And to them rose up the sweet-worded Nestor, the shrill orator of the Pylians,
And words *sweeter than honey* flowed from his tongue."[2]

vii, 38; March 14, 1838

μέροψ ανθρωπος[3]

7. The last half of line 261 has been omitted in the translation here and in *Writings,* I, 66, where the passage also appears.

8. Thoreau gives the English translation both here and with the slightly variant repetition in *ibid.,* i, 96. "θάλασσα 'ηχήεσσα" also appears in *ibid.,* iv, 211.

9. This is the episode of Pallas Athene's coming from heaven to allay Achilles' wrath, told in *Iliad* i, 188–96.

1. This is repeated, *Writings,* i, 65.

2. This is repeated with slight variation, *ibid.,* i, 96.

3. Thoreau uses this expression in connection with Homer, as though it were a quotation. It does not occur, however, in Homer or in Greek in the singular, but in the plural. It would be impossible to name any single use of the expression as Thoreau's source.

VII, 56; August 26, 1838: viii, 555–9

"As when beautiful stars accompany the bright moon through the serene heavens; and the woody hills and cliffs are discerned through the mild light, and each star is visible, and the shepherd rejoices in his heart."[4]

VII, 59; September 7, 1838

When Homer's messengers repair to the tent of Achilles, we do not have to wonder how they get there, but step by step accompany them along the shore of the resounding sea.[5]

VII, 60; October 21, 1838

Hector hurrying from rank to rank is likened to the moon wading in majesty from cloud to cloud.[6]

VII, 60–1; October 21, 1838

We are reminded of the hour of the day by the fact that the woodcutter spreads now his morning meal in the recesses of the mountains, having already laid his axe at the root of many lofty trees.[7]

4. This is a contraction of the Greek original. However, a complete translation of these lines is included in that of lines 553–65 in *Writings*, I, 95–6.
"They, thinking great things, upon the neutral ground of war
Sat all the night; and many fires burned for them.
As when in the heavens the stars round the bright moon
Appear beautiful, and the air is without wind;
And all the heights and the extreme summits,
And the wooded sides of the mountains appear; and from the heavens an infinite ether
    is diffused,
And all the stars are seen; and the shepherd rejoices in his heart;
So between the ships and the streams of Xanthus
Appeared the fires of the Trojans before Ilium.
A thousand fires burned on the plain; and by each
Sat fifty, in the light of the blazing fire;
And horses eating white barley and corn,
Standing by the chariots, awaited fair-throned Aurora."
5. This passage is never directly quoted but is specifically referred to again in *Writings*, I, 96, and *ibid.*, v, 135. The lines suggested are *Iliad* i, 327–8.
6. The passage here referred to is quoted in *Writings*, I, 95:
        "As from the clouds appears the full moon,
           All shining, and then again it goes behind the shadowy clouds,
           So Hector at one time appeared among the foremost,
           And at another in the rear, commanding; and all with brass
           He shone, like to the lightning of aegis-bearing Zeus."
                                  Iliad xi, 62–6.
7. This passage is referred to again in *Writings*, IX, 245, and is quoted, *ibid.*, I, 95:
        "While it was dawn, and sacred day was advancing,
           For that space the weapons of both flew fast, and the people fell;
           But when now the woodcutter was preparing his morning meal,
           In the recesses of the mountain, and had wearied his hands
           With cutting lofty trees, and satiety came to his mind,
           And the desire of sweet food took possession of his thoughts;
           Then the Danaans, by their valor, broke the phalanxes,
           Shouting to their companions from rank to rank."
                                Iliad xi, 84–91.

vii, 61 ; October 23, 1838

Nester's simple repast after the rescue of Machaon is a fit subject for poetry.[8]

vii, 61 ; October 23, 1838 : xii, 278–85

"The snowflakes fall thick and fast on a winter's day. The winds are lulled, and the snow falls incessant, covering the tops of the mountains, and the hills, and the plains where the lotus tree grows, and the cultivated fields. And they are falling by the inlets and shores of the foaming sea, but are silently dissolved by the waves."[9]

vii, 179 ; January 27, 1841

When Venus advanced against the Greeks with resistless valor . . .[1]

vii, 366 ; July, 1845 : xvi, 7, 13–16

"Why are you in tears, Patroclus, like a young child (girl) ?" etc., etc.

> "Or have you only heard some news from Phthia ?
> They say that Menoetius lives yet, son of Actor,
> And Peleus lives, son of Aeacus, among the Myrmidons,
> Both of whom having died, we should greatly grieve."[2]

i, 96 (*The Week;* 1845–49) : xv, 79–84

> "Went down the Idaean mountains to far Olympus,
> As when the mind of a man, who has come over much earth,
> Sallies forth, and he reflects with rapid thoughts,
> There was I, and there, and remembers many things ;
> So swiftly the august Juno hastening flew through the air,
> And came to high Olympus."[3]

i, 96 (*The Week;* 1845–49) : xi, 722–6

"A certain river, Minyas by name, leaps seaward near to Arene, where we Pylians wait the dawn, both horse and foot. Thence with all haste we sped us on the morrow, ere 't was noonday, accoutred for the fight, even to Alphaeus's sacred source," etc.[4]

ii, 101 (*Walden;* 1845–54)

. . . like pygmies we fight with cranes . . .[5]

8. This story, never quoted, is told in the *Iliad* xi, 618–41.

9. This is repeated with slight variation in *Writings*, v, 181–2. It is not a close translation, having been changed from a simile with local details to a generalized description.

1. The source of this is probably the story of Venus' rescue of Aeneas from Diomedes, *Iliad* v, 311 ff. This is, however, a strange description of Venus' very feminine behavior in battle.

2. This is repeated with slight variation in *Writings*, ii, 160.

3. Felton, in his notes on the *Iliad* (p. 444, note to i, 80), speaks of the beauty of this image. He, like Thoreau, translates εἴην, indicative. See *Writings*, xiii, 116: "There was I, and there, and there, as Mercury went down the Idaean mountains." Thoreau has possibly confused the passage referring to Juno with the accounts of Mercury's messenger activities in *Iliad* xxiv.

4. Notice Thoreau's translation of μείναμεν by an English present.

5. This refers to the simile in the opening lines of *Iliad* iii. The same passage is

II, 178 (*Walden;* 1845–54)

Many a lusty crest-waving Hector, that towered a whole foot above his crowding comrades, fell before my weapon and rolled in the dust.[6]

IX, 322; February 27, 1852

—more than a terrestrial river,—which might have suggested that which surrounded the shield in Homer.[7]

XII, 247; May 8, 1854

. . . μέλαινα θάλασσα . . .[8]

IV, 58 ("Cape Cod"; 1855) : xviii, 606

ποταμοῖο μέγα σθένος Ὠκεανοῖο.

IV, 66 ("Cape Cod"; 1855) : i, 34

βῆ δ' ἀκέαν παρὰ θῖνα πολυφλοίσβοιο θαλάσσης[9]

IV, 104 ("Cape Cod"; 1855) : xix, 1–2

"The saffron-robed Dawn rose in haste from the streams
Of Ocean, that she might bring light to immortals and to mortals."

IV, 120 ("Cape Cod"; 1855) : i, 350

Θῖν' ἔφ' ἁλὸς πολιῆς, ὁρόων 'ἐπὶ οἴνοπα πόντον.

IV, 127 ("Cape Cod"; 1855)

The Greeks would not have called the ocean ἀτρύγετος, or unfruitful . . . if they had viewed it by the light of modern science . . .[1]

IV, 149 ("Cape Cod"; 1855) : viii, 485 [2]

Ἐν δ' ἔπεσ' Ὠκεανῷ λαμπρὸν φάος 'ηελίοιο,

IV, 176 ("Cape Cod"; 1855) : vii, 421–3

"The sun once more touched the fields,
Mounting to heaven from the fair flowing
Deep-running Ocean."

---

referred to in *Writings,* II, 178: "A long war, not with cranes, but with weeds, those Trojans who had sun and rain and dews on their side." The comparison is not exactly clear.

6. The adjective κορυθαίολος was one of Homer's favorites for Hector, occurring frequently in the *Iliad.* The falling and rolling in the dust is *Iliad* xxii, 330.

7. Achilles' shield, encircled by the river Oceanus, is described in *Iliad* xviii. Specific mention of the river occurs in lines 606–7.

8. Thoreau's attempt at this time to recall the Homeric words for the dark sea was unsuccessful. Μέλαινα is not used in connection with θάλασσα in the *Iliad.*

9. See also the note here (*Writings,* IV, 66, n. 1) containing the adjective πολυφλοίσβοιος, a common Homeric epithet for the sea, and the expression 'ανάριθμον γέλασμα, which I have not found in Homer. See also *ibid.,* IV, 67: "Reverend Poluphloisboios Thalassa."

1. This is a common epithet for the sea in Homer. However, philologists have now referred the derivation of the word to the root τρυ- rather than to the verb τρυγάω, and it is generally translated "unresting."

2. Thoreau gives an English translation.

IV, 211 ("Cape Cod"; 1855) : xvii, 264–5

> It was the roaring sea, θάλασσα 'ηχήεσσα,—[3]
> ἀμφί δὲ τ' ἄκραι
> 'Ηϊόνες βοόωσιν, ἐρευγομένης ἁλὸς ἔξω.

XVII, 305; November 9, 1858

The body of the victim is delivered up to the children and the dogs and, like the body of Hector, is dragged so many times around Troy.[4]

XVIII, 64; March 19, 1859

I feel somewhat like the young Astyanax at sight of his father's flashing crest.[5]

V, 291 ("Wild Apples")

Ulysses saw in the glorious garden of Alcinoüs "pears and pomegranates, and apple trees bearing beautiful fruit" (καὶ μηλέαι ἀγλαόκαρποι). And according to Homer, apples were among the fruits which Tantalus could not pluck, the wind ever blowing their boughs away from him.[6]

Horace

NOTE: Since the edition of Horace which Thoreau used has not been identified, I have used the one which seems nearest to it (see Supplement to App. A, No. 8). Thoreau's passages show some variations from this text; I have noted the major ones. The first two selections are from Thoreau's *Writings;* the others, from the *College Note-Book (MA. 594)*. Each passage is immediately preceded by identification from the *Odes*. The numbers are for book, ode, and lines.

VII, 106; December, 1839

Odes iii, 29, 54–5: *mea virtute me involvo*

VI, 27; January 23, 1840

Odes i, 9, 1–6: Vides ut alta stet nive candidum
        Nawshawtuct, nec jam sustineant onus
         Silvae laborantes, geluque
         Flumina consteterint acuto?

        Dissolve frigus, ligna super foco
        Large reponens, etc.

Odes i, 4, 3–5: Neque jam stabulis gaudet pecus, aut arator igne,
         Nec prata canis albicant pruinis;
        Jam Cytherea choros ducit Venus imminente luna.

3. This is *Iliad* i, 157. See *Writings*, VII, 33.
4. This incident is found in *Iliad* xxii, 395 ff.
5. This story is told in *ibid.* vi, 467–70.
6. This information is given in *Odyssey* xi, 582–92. The quotation is from line 589. Much derivative material in "Wild Apples" was apparently searched out for the occasion or taken from a secondary source; it does not necessarily indicate reading in the area.

College Note-Book, pp. 55^r–56^r

Odes i, 3, 37–40 : Nil mortalibus arduum est :
  Coelum ipsum petimus stultitiâ ; neque
  Pes nostrum aptimur scelus
  Iracunda Jovem ponere fulmina.

Odes i, 4, 13–15 : Pallida mors aequo pulsat pede pauperum tabernas,
  Regumque turres. O beâte Sexti !
  Vitae summa brevis spem nos vetat inchoare longam.

Odes i, 9, 13–15 : Quid sit futurum cras, fuge quaerere ; et
  Quem sors dierum cumque dabit, lucro
  Appone ;

Odes i, 11, 7–8 : Dum loquimur, fugerit invida
  Aetas ; carpe diem, quam minimum credula postero.

Odes i, 14, 14–15 : Nil pictis timidus navita puppibus
  Fidit :
Odes i, 24, 19–20 : Durum ! sed levius fit patientiâ,
  Quidquid corrigere est nefas.[7]

Odes i, 28, 15–16 : Sed omnes una manet nox,
  Et calcanda semel via leti.

  Ad Apollinem
Odes i, 31, 18–20 : ——dones————
  —nec turpem senectam
  Degere, nec citharâ carentem.

Odes ii, 2, 19–21 : —Virtus, populumque falsis
  Dedocet uti
  Vocibus—

Odes ii, 16, 19–20 : Patriae quis exsul
  Se quoque fugit ?

Odes iii, 3, 1–8 : Justum et tenacem propositi virum
  Non civium ardor prava jubentium,
  Non vultus instantis tyranni
  Mente quatit solida, neque Auster
  Dux inquieti turbidus Adriae,
  Nec fulminantis magna Jovis manus[8]
  Si fractus illabatur orbis,
  Impavidum ferient ruinae.

Odes iii, 4, 65–6 : Vis consillia[9] expers mole ruit suâ ;

7. Thoreau gives this continuously, as though it were one quotation.
8. The transposition here of *manus Jovis* to *Jovis manus* is perhaps Thoreau's greatest variation from the Zeunii text.
9. The text gives *consili.*

Vim temperatam dî quoque provehunt
In majus:

Odes iii, 5, 1–2:	Caelo tonantem credidimus Jovem Regnare—
Odes iii, 5, 29–30:	Nec vera virtus, quum[1] semel excidit, Curat reponi deterioribus

Odes iii, 16, 21–8:	Quanto quisque sibi plura negaverit,
	A dîs plura feret. Nil cupientium
	Nudus castra peto, et transfuga divitum
	    Partes linquere gestio;
	
	Contemptae[2] dominus splendidior rei,
	Quàm si quidquid arat impiger Appulus,
	Occultare meis dicerer horreis,
	    Magnas inter opes inops

Odes iii, 24, 35–6:	Quid leges, sine moribus Vanae, proficiunt?

Odes iii, 29, 41–8:	Ille potens sui
	Laetusque deget—, cui licet in diem
	    Dixisse, "Vixi": cras vel atrâ
	        Nube polum Pater occupato,
	Vel sole puro: non tamen irritum,
	Quodcumque retro est, efficiet; neque
	Diffinget infectumque reddet
	    Quod fugiens semel hora vexit.

Odes iii, 29, 49:	—Fortuna,——————————

Odes iii, 29, 53–6:	si celeres quatit
	Pennas, resigno quae dedit, et meâ
	    Virtute me involvo, probamque
	        Pamperiam sine dote quaero.[3]

Odes iv, 5, 24:	Culpam Poena premit comes[4]
Odes iv, 9, 29–30:	Paulum sepultae distat inertiae *Celata* virtus.[5]

Ovid

NOTE: All references are to Thoreau's *Writings;* all identifications are from the *Metamorphoses*. The numbers are for book and lines. I have used the Delphine Ovid; Thoreau has not followed the text exactly.

1. The text gives *cum*. These four lines are given consecutively by Thoreau.
2. The text gives *contemtae*.
3. It will be noted here that Thoreau's indications of omissions are not dependable.
4. This is followed by Thoreau's note, "Truer than was meant."
5. This is followed by Thoreau's note, *"alio sensu."*

I, 2 (*The Week;* 1845–49) : i, 39–42

> Flumina obliquis cinxit decliva ripis;
> Quae, diversa locis, partim sorbentur ab ipsa;
> In mare perveniunt partim, campoque recepta
> Liberioris aquae pro ripis litora pulsant.[6]

I, 228 (*The Week;* 1845–49) : i, 133–4

> Quaeque diu steterant in montibus altis, Fluctibus ignotis insultavêre carinae;[7]

II, 6 (*Walden;* 1845–54) : i, 414–15

> Inde genus durum sumus, experiensque laborum,
> Et documenta damus quâ simus origine nati.[8]

II, 346 (*Walden;* 1845–54) : i, 61–2; i, 61–2; i, 78–81

> "Eurus ad Auroram, Nabathacaque regna recessit,
> Persidaque, et radiis juga subdita matutinis."

> "The East-Wind withdrew to Aurora and the Nabathaean kingdom,
> And the Persian, and the ridges placed under the morning rays.

. . . . .

> Man was born. Whether that Artificer of things,
> The origin of a better world, made him from divine seed;
> Or the earth, being recent and lately sundered from the high
> Ether, retained some seeds of cognate heaven."

II, 348 (*Walden;* 1845–54) : i, 89–96; i, 107–8

> "The Golden Age was first created, which without any avenger
> Spontaneously without law cherished fidelity and rectitude.
> Punishment and fear were not; nor were threatening words read
> On suspended brass; nor did the suppliant crowd fear
> The words of their judge; but were safe without an avenger.
> Nor yet the pine felled on its mountains had descended
> To the liquid waves that it might see a foreign world,
> And mortals knew no shores but their own.

. . . . .

> There was eternal spring, and placid zephyrs with warm
> Blasts soothed the flowers born without seed."

VIII, 144; 1851 : ii, 254–5; ii, 327–8

> Ovid says:

> > Nilus in extremum fugit perterritus orbem,
> > Occuluitque caput, quod adhuc latet.[9]

6. Thoreau also gives the English translation. He repeats and translates part of the passage in *Writings,* II, 113.

> . . . "campoque recepta
> Liberioris aquae, pro ripis litors pulsant."

7. Thoreau gives the English translation.
8. Thoreau gives Raleigh's poetical translation for this.
9. Thoreau gives the English translation.

Phaëton's epitaph:
　Hic situs est Phaëton currûs auriga paterni;
　Quem si non tenuit, magnis tamen excidit ausis.

VIII, 145; 1851: ii, 349; ii, 363; ii, 377–8; ii, 397; ii, 415; ii, 621–2

His sister Lampetie *subditâ radice retenta est.*

Cortex in verba novissima venit.

　　　　　nec se coeloque, Jovique
Credit, ut injuste missi memor ignis ab illo.[9]

　　　. . . precibusque minas regaliter addit.[9]

Callisto *miles erat Phoebes,* i.e. a huntress.

　　　. . . (neque enim coelestia tingi
Ora decet lachrymis).[9]

VIII, 146; 1851: ii, 728–9

　　　Volat illud, et incandescit eundo;
　　Et, quos non habuit, sub nubibus invenit ignes.[9]

Persius

NOTE: These quotations from Persius come with one indicated exception from the *College Note-Book* (*MA. 594*), pp. 61ʳ–61ᵛ. Part of them occur also in the article on Persius written February 10, 1840, and published in the *Dial* for July, 1840, 1, No. 1, 117–21. The numbers in the identifications refer to satire and lines. Not having the American Delphine edition of Persius and Juvenal which Thoreau had, I have used instead an 1820 London Delphine Persius. Thoreau's quotations vary slightly from this text.

Satires 1, 26–8; 1, 45–9; 1, 63–6

　　　Usq; adeone
Scire tuum nihil est, nisi te scire hoc sciat alter?
At pulchrum est, digito monstrari; et dicier; Hic est.

Non ego, cum scribo, si forte quis aptius exit,
Quando haec rara avis est, si quid tamen aptius exit,
Laudare metuam. Neq; enim mihi cornea fibra est
Sed recti finemque extremumque esse recuso
Euge tuum; et belle.

Quis populi sermo est? Quis enim, nisi carmina molli
Num demum numero fluere, ut per leve severos
Effundat junctura ungues. Scit tendere versum
Non secus ac s'oculo rubricam dirigat uno.

Satires, 2, 6–7

Haud cuivis promptum est, murmurque humilesque susurros
Tollere de templis; et aperto vivere voto.[1]

9. Thoreau gives the English translation.
1. This appears also in the essay written February 10, 1840 (*Writings,* 1, 327–33). It is followed by the English translation.

Satires, 3, 1–2 ; 3, 5–6 ; 3, 32–4 ; 3, 61–3 ; 3, 66, 71–2

Nempe hoc assiduè jam clarum mane fenestras
Intrat, et angustas extendit lumine rimas.

Siccas insana Canicula messes
Iamdudum conquit ; et patula pecus omne sub ulmo est.[2]

Sed stupit hic peteo, et fibris increscit opimum
Pingue : caret culpa : Nescit quid pendat, et alto
Demersus summa rursum non bullit in unda

Est aliquid quo tendis, et in quod dirigis arcum ?
An passim sequeris corvos, testâve, lutove,
Securus quò pes ferat, atque ex tempore vivis ?[8]

Discite – – – – –
Quem te Deus esse
Jussit, et humanâ quâ parte locatus es in re

Satires, 5, 52–3 ; 5, 96–7 ; 5, 104–8

Mille hominum species, et rerum discolor usus.
Velle suum cuique est, nec voto vivitur uno.

Stat contra ratio, et secretam garrit in aurem,
Ne liceat facere id, quod quis vitiabit agendo.[3]

Tibi recto vivere talo
Ars dedit ? Et veri speciem dignoscere calles,
Nequa subaerato mendosum tinneat auro.
Quaeque sequenda forent, et quae vitanda vicissem ;
Illa prius cretâ, mox haec carbone notâsti ?

Writings, II, 327 ; February 10, 1840 : *Satires* prologue, 6–7

"Ipse semipaganus
Ad sacra Vatum carmen affero nostrum."[4]

Varro

NOTE : The references before the colon are to Thoreau's *Writings;* the identifications after the colon are from Varro's *Rerum rusticarum.* The numbers are for book, chapter, and section, or for book and chapter when no section number is needed. Since I could not use the edition of the rustic writers which Thoreau used, I have made the identifications on the basis of the modern Loeb edition.

2. This is followed by Thoreau's note, "This is *all* that could entitle him to the epithet— 'Poet of Nature.' "
3. These appear also in the essay written February 10, 1840 (*Writings,* I, 327–33). They are followed by English translation.
4. Thoreau gives the English translation for this.

I, 382 (*The Week;* 1845–49) : i, 7, 10

> "Caesar Vopiscus Aedilicius, when he pleaded before the Censors, said that the grounds of Rosea were the garden (*sumen,* the tidbit) of Italy, in which a pole being left would not be visible the day after, on account of the growth of the herbage."

XII, 68 : January 14, 1854 : i, 23, 5

> (Varro speaks of planting and cultivating this [a copsewood].[5])

XII, 74 ; January 19, 1854 : i, 1, 9 ; i, 14, 1–4

> Varro, having enumerated certain writers on agriculture, says accidentally [sic][6] that they wrote *soluta ratione,* i.e. in prose.

> Varro divides fences into four kinds,—*unum naturale, alterum agreste, tertium militare, quartum fabrile.* (Many kinds of each.) The first is the living hedge. One kind of *sepes agrestis* is our rail fence, and our other dead wooden farm fences would come under this head. The military *sepes* consists of a ditch and rampart; is common along highways; sometimes a rampart alone. The fourth is the mason's fence of stone or brick (burnt or unburnt), or stone and earth together.

XII, 75 ; January 23, 1854 : i, 13, 2

> Varro speaks of what he calls, I believe, before-light (*antelucana*) occupations in winter, on the farm. Such are especially milking in this neighborhood.

XII, 75 ; January 23, 1854, note to above passage : I, 13, 2

> Speaking of the rustic villa, you must see that the kitchen is convenient, "because some things are done there in the winter before daylight (*antelucanis temporibus*) ; food is prepared and taken."

XII, 81 ; January 27, 1854 : i, 41, 2 ; 1, 46

> Varro, on grafting, says when the wood is of a close and dry texture they tie a vessel over it from which water drops slowly, that the shoot may not dry up before it coalesces ; also "by the turning of some leaves you can tell what season (*tempus*) of the year it is, as the olive and white poplar, and willow. For when their leaves turn, the solstice is said to be past."

XII, 81–2 ; January 27, 1854 : i, 47

> Speaking of the nursery, he says : "Herbaeque elidendae, et dum tenerae sunt vellendae, prius enim aridae factae rixantur, ac celerius rumpuntur, quam sequuntur . . ."[7]

> Contra herba in pratis ad spem foenisiciae nata, non modo non evellenda in nutricatu, sed etiam non calcanda. Quo pecus a prato ablegandum,

---

5. The bracketed insertion is mine.
6. The bracketed insertion is by the editors of the journals.
7. The standard reading here is *soluta oratione.* It is, of course, possible that Thoreau has followed his text.

et omne jumentum, ac etiam homines. Solum enim hominis exitium herbae, et semitae fundamentum.[8]

XII, 82; January 29, 1854: i, 48, 1, 2

Varro says that *gluma* seems to be *a glubendo* because the grain is shelled from its follicle (*deglubitur*). *Arista,* the beard of the grain, is so called because it dries first (*quod arescit prima*). The grain, *granum,* is *a gerendo,* for this is the object of planting, that this may be borne. "But the *spica* (or ear), which the rustics call *speca,* as they have received it from their forefathers, seems to be named from *spes* (hope), since they plant because they *hope* that *this* will be hereafter (*eam enim quod sperant fore*)."[9]

XII, 82–3; January 29, 1854: 1, 2, 14–15

It [the village][1] is from the Latin *villa,* which, together with *via* (a way), or more anciently *vea* and *vella,* Varro derives from *veho* (to carry), because the villa is the place to and from which things are carried. The steward or overseer of the villa was a *vilicus,* and those who got their living by teaming (?) (*vecturis*) were said *vellaturam facere.* And whence the Latin *vilis* and our word *villain* (?).[2]

XII, 89; January 31, 1854: ii, 1, 4–6; ii, 2, 14

Varro thinks that when man reached the pastoral or second stage and domesticated animals (*pecus*), "primum non sine causa putant oves assumptas, et propter utilitatem, et propter placiditatem" (they think not without reason that sheep were first taken, both on account of their usefulness and on account of their gentleness); for, as he says, they furnish milk, cheese, their fleece, and skin. It looks to me as though the sheep had been supplied with a superfluity of clothing that it might share it with man, and, as Varro suggests, did not this fleece, on account of its value, come to be called golden? was not this the origin of the fable?

"Et primitus oritur herba imbribus primoribus evocata," says Varro.[3]

XII, 92; February 3, 1854: iii, 7, 1

Varro speaks of two kinds of pigeons, one of which was wont to alight "on the (*columinibus villae*) columns of a villa (*a quo appellatae columbae*), from which they were called *columbae,* which on account of their natural timidity (*summa loca in tectis captant*) delight in the highest places on the roofs (?) (or under cover?)."

XII, 93: February 4, 1854

Varro says *Africanae bestiae* for savage or ferocious beasts.[4]

8. Thoreau also gives the English translation.
9. A part of this appears also in *Writings,* ii, 184.
1. The bracketed insertion is mine.
2. A passage similar to this appears also in *Writings,* v, 213; "Walking."
3. This appears also in *ibid.,* ii, 343.
4. I have not found this habitual with Varro. One instance of the use is *Rerum rusticarum* iii, 13, 3.

xii, 93 ; February 4, 1854 : ii, 4, 20

Varro speaks of the swineherd accustoming the swine or boars to come at the sound of a horn when he fed them with acorns.

xii, 94 ; February 4, 1854 : ii, 16, 12

As for the locality of beehives, Varro says that they must be placed near the villa, "potissimum ubi non resonent imagines, hic enim sonus harum fugae causa existimatur esse."[5]

xii, 97 ; February 5, 1854 : ii, 11, 10

Even Varro, to prove that the ancients did not shave (or that there were no barbers), is obliged to refer his readers to their statues. "Olim tonsores non fuisse adsignificant antiquorum statuae, quod pleraeque habent capillum, et barbam magnam."

xii, 107 ; February 8, 1854 : ii, introduction, 1 ; ii, introduction, 2, 3 ; iii, 1, 1

And Varro says, "Viri magni nostri majores non sine causa praeponebant rusticos Romanos urbanis. Ut ruri enim, qui in villa vivunt ignaviores, quam qui in agro versantur in aliquo opere faciundo ; sic qui in oppido sederent, quam qui rura colerent, desidiosiores putabant."[5]

And he says that they did not need the gymnasia of the Greeks, but now one does not think that he has a villa unless he has many places with Greek names in it, and, having stolen into the city, instead of using their hands in swinging (?) a scythe or holding a plow they move them in the theatre and circus and have forgotten husbandry.

And in another place V. boasts of the antiquity of rustic life, saying that "there was a time when men cultivated the fields, but had no city (fuit tempus, cum rura colerent homines, neque urbem haberent)."

xii, 107–8 ; February 8, 1854 : iii, 1, 3–4

And again : "Immani numero annorum urbanos agricolae praestant. Nec mirum, quod divina natura dedit agros, ars humana aedificavit urbes.[6]

xii, 108 ; February 8, 1854 : iii, 1, 5

Nec sine causa Terram eandem appellabant matrem, et Cererem, et qui eam colerent, piam et utilem agere vitam credebant, atque eos solos reliquos esse ex stirpe Saturni regis.[6]

xii, 111 ; February 9, 1854 : ii, introduction, 1

After "putabant" in Varro, four pages back, comes "Itaque annum ita diviserunt, ut nonis modo diebus urbanas res usurparent, reliquis vii ut rura colerent (Therefore they so divided the year as to attend to town affairs on the ninth day only, that they might cultivate the fields on the other days)." Hence *nundinae* means a fair, and *oppidum nundinarium*

_____

5. Thoreau gives the English translation.
6. Thoreau gives an English translation here. He repeats the passage in English only in *Writings*, ii, 183.

(a ninth-day town) is a market town, and *forum nundinarium* is the market-place.

XVI, 126; October 25, 1857: ii, 1, 7

I am amused to see that Varro tells us that the Latin *e* represents the vowel sound in the bleat of a sheep (*Bee*).

Vergil

NOTE: The references are to Thoreau's *Writings;* the identifications come from the *Eclogues,* the *Georgics,* and the *Aeneid,* and have, therefore, been individually marked. I have used Thoreau's edition of Vergil for making the identifications; Thoreau's quotations as usual vary slightly from the text.

VII, 11; November 18, 1837: *Eclogues* 6, 84

"Pulsae referunt ad sidera valles" . . .[7]

VII, 12; November 18, 1837: *Eclogues* 6, 8

"agrestam musam,"

VII, 12; November 18, 1837: *Eclogues* 6, 85–6

"Cogere donec oves stabulis, numerumque referre
Jussit, et invito processit Vesper Olympo."

VII, 12; November 20, 1837: *Eclogues* 7, 48

. . . "jam laeto turgent in palmite gemmae,"[8]

VII, 12; November 20, 1837: *Eclogues* 7, 54

. . . "Strata jacent passim sua quaeque sub arbore poma."[9]

VI, 28; January 23, 1840: *Eclogues* 1, 83

Majoresque cadunt altis de montibus umbrae.[1]

VII, 120; February 15, 1840: *Aeneid* vi, 640–1

"Largior hic campos aether et lumine vestit
Purpureo: Solemque suum, sua sidera nôrunt."[2]

v, 138 ("A Walk to Wachusett"; 1842–43): *Aeneid* 1, 7

—atque altae moenia Romae,[3]

7. This is repeated with English translation in *ibid.,* 1, 417.
8. This is repeated with English translation in *ibid.,* 1, 93.
9. This is repeated with English translation in *ibid.* and again with variation but without translation in *ibid.,* 1, 177.
1. This quotation is repeated, extended, and translated in *Writings,* v, 144; "A Walk to Wachusett":
    Et jam procul villarum culmina fumant,
    Majoresque cadunt altis de montibus umbrae.
2. This is repeated without reference to Vergil and with English translation in *Writings,* 1, 406.
3. Thoreau gives the English translation.

v, 138 ("A Walk to Wachusett"; 1842–43) : *Georgics* 1, 130–5

"He shook honey from the leaves, and removed fire,
And stayed the wine, everywhere flowing in rivers;
That experience, by meditating, might invent various arts
By degrees, and seek the blade of corn in furrows,
And strike out hidden fire from the veins of the flint."

I, 257 (*The Week;* 1845–49) : *Georgics* 2, 458

. . . *sua si bona norint* . . .

II, 77 (*Walden;* 1845–54)

It seemed by the distant hum as if somebody's bees had swarmed, and
that the neighbors, according to Virgil's advice, by a faint *tintinnabulum*
upon the most sonorous of their domestic utensils, were endeavoring
to call them down into the hive again.[4]

IV, 91 ("Cape Cod"; 1855)

Or rather he was a sober Silenus, and we were the boys
Chromis and Mnasilus, who listened to his story.[5]

IV, 94 ("Cape Cod"; 1855) : *Eclogues* 6, 74–7

Quid loquar? . . .
            "Aut Scyllam Nisi, quam fama secuta est,
Candida succinctam latrantibus inguina monstris,
Dulichias vexâsse rates, et gurgite in alto
Ah! timidos nautas canibus lacerâsse marinis?"

XIX, 26–7; December 13, 1859: *Georgics* 1, 291–6, 299–308, 310

"Some keep at work by the late light of the winter
Fire, and point torches with a sharp iron,
In the meanwhile the wife, relieving her long labor with her
Singing, thickens the webs with the shrill slay;
Or boils down the liquor of sweet must with fire,
And skims off the foam of the boiling kettle with leaves.

.   .   .   .   .

. . . Winter is an idle time to the husbandman.
In cold weather they commonly enjoy what they have laid up,
And jovial they give themselves up to mutual feasting:
Genial winter invites this and relaxes their cares;
As when now the laden keel has touched its port,
And the joyful sailors have placed a crown on the stern.
However, now is the time to gather acorns,
And laurel berries, and the olive, and bloody (colored) myrtle berries;
Now to set snares for cranes, and deer,
And chase the long-eared hares:

.   .   .   .   .

----

4. The word *tintinnabulum* does not seem to occur in Vergil. Thoreau is possibly
thinking of *Georgics* 4, 64, where the word *tinnitus* occurs in the proper context.
5. This refers generally to *Eclogues* 6.

When the snow lies deep and the rivers are full of drifting ice."

v, 311 ("Wild Apples") : *Eclogues* 1, 81, 82

. . . *mitia poma—, castaneae molles.*

xv, 397 ; June 1, 1857 : *Eclogues* 4, 1

Paulo majora canamus

APPENDIX C

INDEX OF CLASSICAL QUOTATIONS, REFERENCES, AND ALLUSIONS

Prefatory Note

HERE I HAVE collected all classical quotation, reference, and allusion in the twenty volumes of Thoreau's published *Writings*.

Under the entries for classical authors distinction has been made between major pieces of translation, shorter passages of quotation, whether in the original or in English, and simple reference or mention. Under quotation I have put both direct and indirect quotation. Occasionally it has been difficult to distinguish clearly between a very indirect quotation of a certain classical passage and a rather full reference to it. In such cases, if any appreciable part of the actual phrasing of the original passage occurs, I have classified it as a quotation whether Thoreau so acknowledged it or not.

Brackets have been used for two different purposes: to mark quotations for which Thoreau gave no indication of source and to indicate hidden references. That is, a quotation from Homer which is not acknowledged by Thoreau as Homer is entered under *Homer* and bracketed. A reference to "Phthian hero, vulnerable in heel," appears not only under *Phthian hero* but in brackets under *Achilles*. Absyrtus is referred to by Thoreau twice but never by name; therefore the name itself appears in brackets in the index.

Adjectives derived from nouns are entered under the noun entry, with whatever additional notation is necessary for clarity. Under the entry *Greece* (*Grecian* ──), a volume and page number followed by no additional information means simply that the base word *Greece* appears in that location. Volume and page number followed by *cities* means that the expression *Grecian cities* occurs in that location. Volume and page number followed by *also cities* means that not only does the base word *Greece* occur in that place but the expression *Grecian cities* also occurs on the same page.

A classical reference which is not actually attributable to Thoreau is followed by the source to which it can be attributed. (*Gesner*) after an entry means that the reference was derived from Gesner; (*in Gesner*) means that the reference actually occurs in a quotation from Gesner. (*Gesner and in Gesner*) indicates that the entry occurs both in connection with and in quotation from Gesner. In a few cases where I have known the reference to be secondary or quoted but have not known the source I have used the notations (*secondary*) or (*in quotation*).

It is impossible to guarantee the completeness of an index. However, a comparison of this index with the general indices of the published works will give some indication of the thoroughness with which this one has been compiled.

[Absyrtus], VII, 108; 480
Academus grove, VII, 29

---

1. Classical references within this play have not been indexed.

Amyntas, VII, 57; 233[2]

Anacreon:
Quoted from: XI, 13
Referred to: V, 107; VII, 464; IX, 319; XV, 323
Translations from: I, 238–44;[3] V, 108; 109–10; VII, 66–7; 69–70

Anchises, I, 136 (Ross); IX, 96

Antaeus, II, 171; VII, 187; 372, Antaeus-like; 393; VIII, 204, Antaeus-like;
IX, 107, Antaeus-like; X, 197; XVIII, 89; 353

Antigone, I, 139 (quoted from Sophocles' *Antigone*)

Antinoüs, XII, 56 (in Gilpin)

Apollo (*see also* Phoebus and Phoebus Apollo), I, 64 (in Hesiod); 65; 66;
96 (Homer); 211; [III, 143]; VI, 39; 44; VII, 32; 175; 391; 393 (Ross);
VIII, 373; 378; IX, 5; X, 114; XI, 379; XII, 56, Apollo Belvidere; XVII, 424;
XVIII, 95 (Pindar); 130

Appian Way, VII, 84

Arcadia, I, 257, Arcadian lives; II, 63; VII, 19, *Arcadians;* VIII, 454, *also*
Arcady

[Archilochus], I, 176; 334[4]

Archimedes, IV, 290; VIII, 17

Arene, I, 96 (in Homer)

Arethuse, I, 401; IV, 322

Argo, III, 35; 137; IV, 140

Argonautic expedition, IV, 140–1; V, 111; VII, 483

Argonauts, I, 61; 258 (Pindar); 346

Argus, I, 135

Ariadne, I, 399 (Chaucer)

Aristaeus, I, 57 (in Lydgate); *ibid.,* (Ross); VII, 394 (Ross)

Aristophanes:
Referred to: XIX, 195

Aristotle:
Quoted from:[5] I, 133; 386; VII, 139; VIII, 150 (in Cudworth)
Referred to: V, 111 (in Nuttall); VII, 35; 150 (Cudworth); 171; 440 (in
de Gerando); XI, 5; XV, 299 (Agassiz);[6] XVIII, 372, Aristotelean
method; XIX, 55; 77

Aspasis, VII, 397 (Landor)

Astyanax, XVIII, 64 (Homer)

Atalanta, V, 316; [IX, 84]

---

2. Amyntas is a shepherd in Vergil's *Eclogues* 3, 5, and 10. Faustus is mentioned by
Thoreau with Amyntas. The only Faustus in classical literature is an obscure poet mentioned in Juvenal. Thoreau must have meant Faustulus.

3. These translations have all been indexed for interior reference.

4. These are references to the popular translation of the Archilochian fragment, "He
who fights and runs away, May live to fight another day." Thoreau may not even have
known that it was from Archilochus.

5. These fragmentary quotations from Aristotle might have come from any number
of secondary sources. There is no reason to believe that Thoreau actually read Aristotle's
philosophical works.

6. This was from a conversation with Agassiz.

Athenians, I, 265; VII, 19; 164; 370, Athenian mob; XIX, 151, an Athenian
   (in Gesner)
Athens, I, 100 (Quarles); 264; 266, Athenian glory; VII, 26; X, 458; XIX,
   151[7]
Atlantides, I, 278 (title of original poem); VII, 77
Atlantis, II, 329; IV, 178; V, 219; IX, 186; XI, 216; XII, 74
Atlas, II, 93; III, 70; VI, 243; 362
Atridae, I, 240 (in Anacreon)
Atropos, II, 131
Attic ——, I, 319, salt; VI, 345, salt; VII, 93, life; 140, bee; 141, salt
Attica, IV, 284[8]
Augean stables, II, 5; VII, 427
Augustan Age, IV, 332, ages; V, 232; XII, 68
Augustine, St.:
   Quoted from: V, 329 (in Raleigh)
   Referred to: XIV, 203
Augustus, XIX, 17 (in Pliny)
Aurora, I, 61; 199; [267] (in original poem); II, 40; 98; 99; 154; 346 (in
   Ovid); IV, 174; V, 399, "The Aurora of Guido" (title of original poem);
   VII, 85 (in original poem); 167, of Guido; XVI, 364
Autumnus, VI, 38

Bacchanal, XI, 356; 394
Bacchantes, I, 360
Bacchus, I, 58 (Ross); V, 110 (in Anacreon); VII, 69 (in Anacreon); 393
   (Ross); XVIII, 314
Balearian sling, VIII, 145 (Ovid)
Bards (as part of Druidical order), VII, 18[9]
Battus, I, 258 (Pindar)
Bias, [II, 27]; VII, 169; 169–70
Boethius:
   Referred to: VII, 289[1]
Boreas, I, 257; V, 183, Boreal leisure; VII, 45; 51 (in original poem); IX, 175,
   boreal spirit
Bosphorus, VIII, 19
Briareus, I, 135

Cadmus, I, 240 (in Anacreon); V, 239; XII, 133
Caelum (as mythological personification), XI, 347

7. This reference is in parentheses in a quotation from Gesner. I take it to be Thoreau's
interpolation, but I have not thought it necessary to search through Gesner to verify
this.
   8. In quotation as in indirect statement of Columella.
   9. Neither this material nor the Latin quoted under "Saxons," *Writings,* VII, 20,
seems to have a classical source.
   1. Thoreau also copied from Alfred's *Boethius* into the commonplace book *HM957*
in Huntington Library. He apparently met Boethius in the study of Anglo-Saxon rather
than in Latin.

---

2. I have not included references to a Negro named Cato.

3. Both of these quotations are so common that it is probably unnecessary to refer
them to Cicero.

4. Since there is no evidence that Thoreau read Theocritus, this is probably a Vergilian echo.
5. In quotation from a nonclassical source.
6. This episode is probably from Homer, *Iliad* v.
7. Partly quoted from nonclassical source.

Egeria, VII, 298
Elean youths, VII, 187
Eleusis, VII, 219; 483, Eleusinian mysteries
Empedocles, VII, 139 [8]
Endymion, I, 58 (Ross); V, 326; 331; VII, 121; VIII, 495; X, 226
Enna, X, 94
Epeians, I, 96 (Homer)
Epicurus:
  Quoted from: VII, 150 (Cudworth)
Erebus, VIII, 489
Erymanthian boar, VII, 427
Eschines, VII, 397 (Landor)
Etruria, I, 176, Etruscan story; 265; 360, Etruscans; V, 133, Etrurian hills; VIII, 159
Eubulides, VII, 397 (Landor)
Eumenides, I, 59 (Ross)
Euphemus, I, 258 (Pindar)
Euripides:
  Quoted from: IV, 301; VII, 139 [9]
Eurus, II, 346 (in Ovid); VII, 51 (in original poem)
Eurypylus, I, 258 (Pindar)
Euterpeans, XV, 245

Falernian wine, VII, 60 (in original poem)
Fates, IV, 352; V, 403 (in original poem); VI, 74; 108; VIII, 6
Fauns, VII, 393 (Ross)
Faunus, XIII, 27
Furies, IV, 352

Galen, X, 86 (in Evelyn)
Geryon, VII, 427
Golden fleece, I, 135; VII, 130; XII, 89 (Varro)
Gorgon-like, II, 89 (in Carew)
Gracchus, Gaius, XIX, 16–17 (in Pliny)
Gracchus, Tiberius, XIX, 16 (in Pliny)
Graces, I, 59 (Ross); 109; V, 109 (in Anacreon); VII, 69 (in Anacreon); XII, 70 (in Anacreon)
Greece (Grecian ——), I, 15, cities (in original poem); 54 (in original poem); 65; *also* gods; 96; 102; 164; 264, valor; 265; 266; 345; 346; 366; II, 78, style of architecture; 113, *also* multitude; 114, literature; 240; IV, 339, sky (in Schiller translated by Carlyle); V, 107; 109; 229; 231; 232, mythology; 292; 331, epithet; 404–5 (in original poem); VI, 55, Grecians; VII, 19; 29; 33; 61; 68, era; 105, Grecians (in Plutarch); 142, light; 165, history; 167; 168; 281; 283; 361, 363, art; 365; 391, fables; 425, games;

8. This quotation is one of a collection of epigrams; it probably came from some non-classical, philosophical source.
9. See n. 8, above. This quotation came from Euripides' *Orestes,* but there is no evidence that Thoreau ever read the play.

---

1. I cannot discover any real evidence that Thoreau ever read Hesiod.

2. From marginal index in Benzo's *History of the West Indies*.

3. From Ricketson's shanty walls.

4. These references are for mention of the *Iliad* only; all quotations from the *Iliad* are indexed under Homer.

5. No actual fragments of Latin have been indexed here; these are references containing the word "Latin" or some derivative of the word.

Lyaeus (Bacchus), I, 241 (in Anacreon)
Lycurgus, I, 360; IV, 478; VIII, 47
Lydian ——, VII, 214, shaft; VII, 392, music (Ross)

Machaon, VII, 61 (Homer)
Mantua, I, 49
Marathon, I, 54 (in original poem); V, 404 (in original poem); VII, 98
Mars, III, 8, Mars' Hill, Mars' field; VII, 392; XII, 72, Mars Sylvanus (Cato)
Marsyas, VII, 392 (Ross); 393 (Ross)
Meander, I, 235 (in original poem); XVIII, 390
Medea, VII, 108
Medusa, XI, 45; XV, 175
Megareans, I, 265; VII, 164 (-ians)
Melibaeus, V, 311 (Vergil)
Memnon, I, 58 (Ross); 185; 267 (in original poem); II, 40; 99; VII, 376 (in
    original poem); 386; XVIII, 301, Memnonian music
Menander:
    Referred to: I, 238; IX, 219; 319
Menoetius, II, 160 (in Homer); VII, 366 (in Homer)
Mercury, V, 402 (in original poem); IX, 12; XIII, 116 (Homer)
Mimnermus:
    Referred to: I, 238; IX, 319
Mincius, VI, 92
Minerva, I, 65; 79; 264; II, 37 (Ross); 265; V, 125; [291]; VII, 165; 393
    (Ross)
Minos, VII, 391 (Ross)
Minotaur, IV, 437
Minyas, I, 96 (in Homer)
Mnasilus, IV, 91 (Vergil)
Momus, II, 37 (Ross)
Musaeus, I, 238
Myrmidons, II, 160 (in Homer); 253 (Homer); VII, 366 (in Homer)

Naiads (Naiades), I, 86; VII, 85 (in original poem); X, 200
Narcissus, I, 58 (Ross)
Nearchus, IV, 215
Nemean lion, VII, 427
Nemesis, I, 59; VII, 242; X, 157; 158
Neptune,[6] I, 57 (in Ross); IV, 58; 68; VI, 28; VII, 47; 393 (Ross); XIII,
    136 (quotation)
Nereids, XI, 28
Nereus, V, 126; VII, 271
Nero, VIII, 173 (De Quincey and in De Quincey)
Nervii, II, 285
Nestor, I, 66 (Homer); 96 (Homer); VII, 31 (Homer); 33 (in Homer);

6. I have omitted reference to Louis Neptune, the Indian, and to the river steamer *Governor Neptune*.

[34] (Homer) ; 61 (Homer) ; VIII, 449; IX, 20, Nestorian Christians
Night (as mythological personification), III, 78; IV, 78
Numa, IV, 278; 478; VIII, 47

Oceanides, I, 166
Odyssey,[7] II, 98; IX, 270
Oedipus, VII, 237 (interpretation of Emerson's "The Sphinx") ; XV, 372
 Sophocles' *Oedipus at Colonus*)
Oenoean stag, VII, 427
Olympia, I, 102; 103, Olympian bards (in Emerson) ; 346, Olympic games ;
 VI, 55; VII, 187, Olympian youths
Olympus, I, 96 (in Homer) ; 408, Olympian land (in original poem) ; II, 94;
 III, 140; V, 133; VI, 93; 179; VII, 12 (in Vergil) ; 29; 55; 361; 374, Olympic
 land (in original poem) ; XI, 200; 360; 360–1, Mt. Olympus
Onescritus, I, 137
Opimius Lucius, XIX, 17 (in Pliny)
Oreads, I, 86
Orestes, IV, 301, quotation from Euripides' *Orestes;* [8] [IV, 339] (in transla-
 tion from Schiller) ; VII, 113
Origen, VII, 133 (in Cudworth)
Orpheus,[9] I, 50; 97; 98; 238; 346; 363; II, 187; III, 138; VI, 268; IX, 183,
 Orphean fashion of building; 219; 235; 255; X, 23, Orphean fashion of
 saw mill; XII, 193; XVIII, 128; 130
Ossa, I, 86; VI, 220
Ostia, I, 39
Oswald's *Etymological Dictionary,* V, 138
Ouates (as part of Druidical order), VII, 18 [1]
Ovid :
 Quoted from : I, 2; [113] ; [228] ; II, [6] ; [346] ; [348] ; IV, 157 (in Sir
 Thomas Browne in Brand's *Popular Antiquities*) ; VIII, 144–6

Pactolus, IX, 95
Paestum, VI, 55 (in original poem)
Palinurus, VII, 27
Palladius :
 Quoted from : V, 294; 308
 Referred to : XII, 55, Palladian architecture (in Gilpin) ; XIV, 329
Pallas Athene, VII, 33 (Homer)
Palmyra, V, 172
Pan, I, 58 (Ross) ; 65, *also* Pantheon ; 360, Panathenaea ; III, 138, Pandaean
 pipes

7. These references are for mention of the *Odyssey* only; any quotations from the
Odyssey are listed under Homer.
8. Since this occurs in a list of quotations (*Writings,* VII, 139), it is probably from
some other source than the *Orestes.*
9. These are all mentions of Orpheus, the mythological inventor of music; there are
no quotations from the pseudo-Orpheus in the published writings.
1. This reference seems to come from a nonclassical source.

2. These selections have not been indexed for interior reference.

Plato:

Quoted from: I, 183–4 (in Plutarch) ; IV, 304 (in Raleigh) ; VII, 105 (in Plutarch)

Referred to: I, 105 ; 159 (Cudworth) ; 279: II, 119 ; 165 ; IV, 345 ; VI, 113 ; 146 ; 150 ; 153 ; VII, 19 ; 121 ; 150 (Cudworth) ; 171 ; 352 ; 369 ; 440 (de Gerando) ; VIII, 150 (Cudworth) ; IX, 256 ; XI, 5 ; XII, 209

Pliny:

Quoted from: IV, 216 ; V, 292 ; 295 ; 299 ; 323 ; [IX, 273] ; XIX, 16–17 ; 152 (in Gesner) ; XX, 310

Referred to: IV, 215 ; V, 280 ; VIII, 168 ; IX, 118 (Stoever) ; 229 (in Lindley in Loudoun) ; X, 86 (in Evelyn) ; XV, 496 (in Loudoun) ; XIX, 104 ; 133 ; XX, 329 ; 331, n. 1

Plotinus:

Quoted from: V, 329 (in Raleigh) ; VII, 139³

Plutarch:

Quoted from: I, [79] ;⁴ 183–4 ; [265] ;⁴ VII, 100 ;⁵ [105] ; 105–6 ; [164] ;⁴ [165] ⁴

Referred to: I, 320 (in original poem) ; IV, 350 ; IX, 239 ; XVIII, 403

Pluto, *v*, 122 ; 164

Plutus, II, 183

Po, IV, 481

Polynices, I, 139 (Sophocles)

Pomona, v, 295 ; 298 (in quotation) ; VII, 372 ; VIII, 383 ; X, 67

Pomponius Secundus, XIX, 16 (in Pliny)

Priene, VII, 169

Prometheus, I, 59 (Ross) ;⁶ 60 ; 67 ; III, 70 ; 260, *Prometheus Bound;* IV, 338, Promethean flames ; v, 156 ; Promethean energy ; 337–75 ; translation of *Prometheus Bound;* VIII, 390 ; [IX, 111] ; XI, 231 ; XIV, 312 (Lucretius)

Proserpine: I, 18 ; X, 81 ; 92 ; 94 ; 193 ; XIX, 397

Proteus, III, 59 ; IV, 68 ; 118 ; VII, 130 ; IX, 437 ; X, 150, Protean character of water lights ; XI, 28 ; XII, 70

Pylades, VII, 113

Pylians, I, 96 (Homer and in Homer) ; VII, 33 (in Homer)

Pyrrha, II, 6 (Ovid)

Pythagoras:

Quoted from: I, 71–2 ; 184–5 ; 338 (all in Jamblichus)

Referred to: I, 105 ; 137 ; 159 (Cudworth) ; II, 179, is himself a Pythagorean ; VII, 150 (Cudworth) ; 352 ; 413 ; VIII, 213

Pythian priestess, VII, 126

Pythias, VII, 113 ; XVI, 127

---

3. This quotation appears in a page of mottoes and is almost surely from a secondary source.

4. These are probably, but not certainly, from Plutarch.

5. This is identified in the published journal as Plutarch, *Morals* "Roman Questions" lxviii. It is lxxviii.

6. I list this as referable to Ross because it is included with much other material from Ross. Most of Thoreau's interest in Prometheus is probably referable to Aeschylus.

Remus, [II, 5] ; V, 224; VII, 22; [428] ; VIII, 151

Rhadamanthus, VII, 391 (Ross)

Rhodes, I, 81 ; 259 (Pindar) ; [XVIII, 95]

Rome, Roman ——, I, 15, Romes, *also* Roman worth (in original poem) ;
    106, Roman army; 264, Roman story; 265; 266; 345, *also* Roman time
    standard; 346; 358; 395 (in Chaucer) ; II, 10, Roman praetors (in
    Evelyn) ; 113, *also* Roman multitude; 179; 240; 365; IV, 16; 278; 328,
    Roman character (writing) ; 440; V, 138 (in Vergil) ; 139; 229; 231 ; 236,
    Roman army; 287; 294, Roman writer; 409, Roman state (in original
    poem) ; VI, 25, Roman pronunciation; 67 ; 153, Roman soldier ; 342, Roman
    nose; VII, 22; 26 ; 84, Roman forum; 171, Roman greatness; 192; 266;
    283; 353, Roman army; 365; 390, Roman story; 409 (in original poem) ;
    454; VIII, 70; 144; 151; 159, *also* Roman empire; 173 (De Quincey) ;
    182, Roman Saturnalia; 210; Roman army; 346; 404, Roman soldier;
    418, Roman aqueduct; 444, *also* Roman life, farmers, kitchen, nation, peo-
    ple (Cato) ; 445, Roman agriculturalists, history (Cato) ; 446, Roman
    family (Cato) ; 494; X, 86, *also* Roman provinces (in Evelyn) ; 109; 214,
    Roman emperor; XI, 223, Roman peasantry; 331, Roman house; XII, 62;
    XIII, 20, Roman aqueduct; XIV, 229, *also* Roman authors; XVI, 93, Roman
    style of architecture; XVII, 423 ; XVIII, 445, Roman history; XX, 57 (Shake-
    speare)

Roman (a, the, Romans), I, 40, a Roman; 264, the Roman, the Romans;
    305, Romans (in quotation) ; 365, a Roman; II, 183, the Romans (Varro) ;
    276–7, Roman, Romans (Varro) ; IV, 54, later Romans (Indians) ; 448,
    Romans; V, 222, 223, Romans; VI, 67, Romans; VII, 23, the Romans;
    165, Romans; 198, a Roman; 370, the Roman; 390, Romans, the Roman;
    VIII, 173, Romans (De Quincey) ; 418, the Romans; 445, Romans (Cato) ;
    450, the Roman (Cato), the Romans (Cato) ; XI, 223, a Roman; XII,
    69, Romans (Cato); 107, Romans (in Varro) ; 111, Romans; 112,
    farmer Romans (Columella) ; XIV, 229, 288, the Romans; 387, Romans;
    XVI, 136, Romans; XVIII, 454, Romans; XIX, 16, Romans

Romulus, [II, 5] ; V, 224; VII, 22; [428] ; VIII, 151

Rubicon, IV, 308; XI, 147; 187

Sacred way, VII, 84

Salamis, I, 265; IV, 250; VII, 164

Sardanapalus, II, 40; IX, 191

Saturn, II, 183 (in Varro) ; VII, 391 ; VIII, 285; XI, 230; XII, 108 (in Varro) ;
    XVIII, 349

Saturnalia, VIII, 182; XI, 331

Satyrs, VIII, 187; 393 (Ross)

Satyrus, XIII, 27

Scamander, I, 10; VI, 93

Scipio Africanus, II, 284

Seneca:
    Quoted from:[7] I, 407; IV, 436; VI, 219; XV, 218; XVIII, 435

7. This passage comes through Daniel. I suspect that Thoreau knew it as Daniel and
not as Seneca.

Thamyris, VII, 392 (Ross) ; 393 (Ross)
Thebes, I, 128; 241 (in Anacreon) ; II, 64; v, 74; VI, 102 (Aeschylus' *Seven against Thebes;* VII, 357 (Lydgate's *Story of Thebes*) ; 392 (Ross) ; x, 153
Theophrastus:
   Referred to: v, 291 ; 292; IX, 118; XIX, 133; 240
Thera, I, 258 (Pindar)
Thermopylae, v, 405 (in original poem) ; VII, 216; IX, 149
Theseus, II, 89 (in Carew)
Thessalian hills, v, 133
Thracian bard, IV, 91 (in Scott)
Tiber, v, 171 ; VIII, 173 (in Juvenal in De Quincey)
Tiberius, VIII, 173 (in Blackwell in De Quincey)
[Tibullus] :
   Quoted from: II, 191
Titan, I, 202 (in Fletcher) ; 406, Titans; III, 70, Titanic scenery; 71, Titanic nature; 79; IV, 331, Titanian (in Carlyle) ; 345, Titans; v, 55, Titans; 110 (in Anacreon) ; VII, 69 (in Anacreon) ; VIII, 258; x, 22, Titanic (of (fire) ; 156 Titanic force; xv, 277; xx, 40, 41, Titans
Tityrus, v, 311
Triton, I, 258 (Pindar) ; v, 126; VII, 130; 271; XI, 28
Troglodytes, VII, 373 (in original poem)
Troy, I, 10 (in Chaucer) ; 95, Trojans (in Homer) ; 136; 241 (in Anacreon) ; 320 (in original poem) ; 346, Trojan war; 411 ; II, 49; 178, Trojans; 214, Trojan horse; VII, 31 (Homer) ; 52; 219; IX, 245 (Homer) ; XI, 266, Trojan horse; XVII, 305 (Homer)
Tullus Hostilius, VIII, 324 ; XII, 28
Tuscan villa, I, 301 ; VII, 283; 348
Tydeus, VII, 116 (Aeschylus)
Tyrian dye, IV, 193 ; v, 273, Tyrian purple; VII, 101
Tyrrhenian mariners, I, 58 (Ross) ; VII, 393 (Ross)
Tyrtaean tones, IX, 219

Ulysses, II, 108; v, 291 (Homer) ; VII, 363

Varro:
   Quoted from: I, 382; II, 183; [184] ; [343] ; v, 213; XII, 74; 75; 81; 81–2; 82; 82–3; 89; 92; 93; 94; 97; 107–8; 111
   Referred to: XII, 68; 111 (Columella) ; 114; XVI, 126
Venus, I, 65; 244 (in Anacreon) ; [v, 291] ; VII, 70 (in Anacreon) ; 179 (Homer) ;[8] 181, Venus de Medici; 391 ; 392; [IX, 84] ; XII, 56
Vergil:
   Quoted from: I, 93; [177][9] [257] ; [406] ; [417] ; [IV, 94] ; v, 138; 144; [311] ; [VI, 28] ; VII, 11–12; 120; x, 86 (in Evelyn) ; XIV, 56 (in Columella) ; [xv, 397] ; XIX, 26–7

8. This is told both in Homer and in Vergil, but Thoreau's source was probably Homer.
9. This is a variation of Vergil.

Referred to: I, 122; 327; 396; II, 115; 177; IV [91]; 328; V, 133; 143; 317 (Bodaeus); VII, [57]; [121]; [233]; 311; 369; IX, 134–5, *Sortes Virgilianae;* 328; 424; XII, 114; 434; XV, 324; 496 (in Loudoun); XIX, 17 (in Pliny)

Vesper, VII, 12 (in Vergil)

Vesta, II, 69, vestal fire; IV, 278; XII, 72 (Cato)

Vesuvius, IV, 481; V, 331 (in Richter)

Virginia, I, 399 (Chaucer)

Vitruvius, II, 64; III, 138; VII, 281

Vopiscus (Caesar Vopiscus Aedilicius), I, 382 (in Varro)

Vulcan, I, 240 (in Anacreon); II, 275; III, 70; 140; VI, 28; 39; VII, 167; 386. 451; X, 22; XII, 194, Vulcanic force)

Xanthus, I, 10; 95 (in Homer); 235 (in original poem)

Xenophon:
Referred to: I, 228; 319; VII, 27; 141

Zeno, VII, 26–7 (Lemprière)

Zephyr, I, 245; VII, 50 (in original poem); 86, Zephyrus (in original poem); IX, 175, zephyral spirit; XI, 294

Zeus, I, 95 (in Homer); [96] (Homer); 259 (Pindar)

Supplement to Appendix C

Many Latin and Greek words and many fragments of Latin and Greek quotation appear in Thoreau's *Writings*. They have little importance, and they fit into no particular categories. Here I have gathered those which have not found a place elsewhere: such expressions as *Memento mori,* as *Veni, vidi, vici,* as *terra firma;* a few isolated and unidentified quotations; a few experiments in philology. I have however, refused to catalog *via, versus,* and purely botanical and zoological terms.

LATIN:

Writings, I, 100, 113, 122, 175, 176, 177, 198, 328, 330, 398; II, 7, 69, 73, 90, 173, 231, 253, 276, 297, 325, 326, 338–9, 349, 362; III, 7, 220; IV, 4, 32, 38 (n. 1), 55, 79, 161, 178, 179, 187–8, 202, 236, 249, 289, 330, 331, 333, 344, 350, 358, 435, 472; V, 73, 89, 101, 139, 179, 185, 207, 211, 219, 221, 222–3, 228, 278, 315, 316–17, 317; VI, 20, 27–9, 140, 176, 207, 208, 243, 322, 378; VIII, 81, 87, 168, 170, 173, 174, 222, 223, 289, 293, 404, 495; IX, 108, 118, 134, 135, 219, 271, 272, 272–3, 275, 307, 316, 324, 349, 408, 446–8, 461; X, 72, 152, 158; XI, 62, 83, 145, 284, 459; XIII, 139; XIV, 130, 451; XV, 323, 384, 397, 398; XVI, 79, 110, 297; XVII, 452; XVIII, 438; XIX, 151, 168, 268; XX, 262, 273

GREEK:

Writings, I, 98, 239, 389, 406, 419; II, 338–9; IV, 178, 198, 269; V, 240, 291; VI, 243; VIII, 150; IX, 97, 108, 272; XII, 247; XVI, 53, 127; XIX, 10, 55, 151

INDEX

*Footnote source references to the journals have not been indexed.

†Footnote source references to Walden and The Week have not been indexed.